Inquiry and the Literary Text

Constructing Discussions in the English Classroom

Classroom Practices in Teaching English
Volume 32

Edited by

James Holden
St. Olaf College

John S. Schmit
Augsburg College

National Council of Teachers of English
1111 W. Kenyon Road, Urbana, Illinois 61801-1096

Staff Editor: Tom Tiller

Interior Design: Doug Burnett

Cover Design: Pat Mayer

NCTE Stock Number 23430-3050

It is the policy of NCTE in its journals and other publications to provide a fo-rum for the open discussion of ideas concerning the content and the teaching of English and the language arts. Publicity accorded to any particular point of view does not imply endorsement by the Executive Committee, the Board of Directors, or the membership at large, except in announcements of policy, where such endorsement is clearly specified.

Although every attempt is made to ensure accuracy at the time of publication, NCTE cannot guarantee that all published addresses for electronic mail or Web sites are current.

Countee Cullen's "Yet Do I Marvel," from *On These I Stand,* is reprinted in Chapter 9 by permission. Copyrights held by Amistad Research Center. Ad-ministered by Thompson and Thompson, New York, NY.

Library of Congress Catalog Card Number 85-644740

ISBN 0-8141-2343-0
ISSN 0550-5755

For our mothers, Esther Sorlie Holden and Eraine Schmit, talented teachers both inside the classroom and outside, who inspired us with a love of learning.

Contents

III. Strategies for Assessing Inquiry-Based Approaches

Preface

The idea for this book was born out of an interest we two editors share—using Socratic or Paideia seminars to facilitate discussions of literature. However, we soon realized that a broader approach might best serve our presumed audience of secondary English teachers, so we decided to focus on an inquiry approach to constructing discussions in the classroom. Therefore, we begin this preface by discussing what the term *inquiry* means to us. According to the *American Heritage Dictionary*, the word has three definitions: "1. The act of inquiring, 2. A question; query, 3. A close examination of some matter in a quest for information or truth." (See the first page of the chapter by Jacqueline Thursby in this book for another definition of *inquiry*.) For the purposes of this book, it is this quest for information or truth by thoughtful questioning (either by a teacher or by the students) that we are advocating, a quest that John Dewey describes as "**reflective inquiry** in which the thinker turns a subject over in the mind, giving it serious and consecutive consideration" (qtd. in Friedman 96 [boldface in original]).

Some would say inquiry involves using a contextual teaching approach, one that is rooted in students' real lives as family members, citizens, workers, or students (see Beach and Myers). We have seen inquiry learning strategies employed in such models as the open school popularized in the 1960s, in problem-based learning, in research-based learning, in project-based learning, and in process writing approaches. More recently we have seen this approach used in classrooms where teachers employ cooperative learning and reader-response models. Given this background, it is our strongly-held belief that students are not simply blank slates that we English teachers write on; rather, they are thoughtful and knowledgeable human beings who have the ability, with proper guidance, to explore texts in ways we cannot imagine. Joseph Auciello, in a March 2000 *English Journal* article, states this notion in these words:

> There are no blank slates. Since all readers look at a literary work through their own lenses and interpret that work within the unique context of their lives, a good English class does not aspire to uniformity. Such a classroom does not require every student to think the same thoughts about the same book. Difference of opinion is actually a virtue in literary study, since it can lead to a deepening of thought when one person's idea expands by consideration of other ideas (91).

In order then to create such a classroom—call it an inquiry classroom if you will—one needs a tactic or approach that gives students a voice. As we considered approaches to inquiry that might be most appropriate for our readers, we thought about a best practices focus. In fact, many of the thirteen principles of best practice are represented in the chapters of this book: student-centered, experiential, holistic, authentic, expressive, reflective, social, collaborative, democratic, cognitive, developmental, constructivist, challenging ("13 Principles of Best Practice" 5; see also Zemelman, Daniels, and Hyde). For example, many of the chapters begin with the premise that students should investigate their own questions *(student-centered);* others emphasize active, hands-on, concrete experience *(experiential);* some encourage the use of a variety of communicative media *(expressive);* and still others focus on the socially constructed, interactional nature of learning *(social).* Above all, these educators encourage students to be *reflective inquirers*, often in a *collaborative* or cooperative setting; and several chapters describe *constructivist* notions of learning. In the end, we have tried to provide some historical and theoretical background on the topic, give readers specific strategies for structuring inquiry discussions of literature in their classrooms, and include essays about assessing inquiry-based approaches.

Chapter 1, by James Holden, provides a brief historical overview of inquiry teaching methods (beginning with Socrates and his dialogues), identifies some of Socrates' modern descendants, discusses one type of Socratic seminar, mentions several influential books about inquiry teaching (most notably Louise Rosenblatt's *Literature as Exploration)*, and concludes by identifying some inquiry models used in classrooms today.

The first section of the book, Strategies for Inquiring into Texts, includes six "how-to-do-it-tomorrow" chapters. If you are eager to hand over the job of creating discussion questions to your students, you will want to pay particular attention to Chapter 2, "Master Questions and the Teaching of Literature," in which Mark Gellis outlines a student-centered, active-learning approach to teaching literature to students whom he calls novice readers. It is an approach which focuses on asking questions and encouraging personal responses. Students first respond to the text with a short reaction essay and generate questions about the text for class discussion, using a set of strategies for exploring literary texts. These strategies are noted in a chapter appendix titled "Playing Twenty Questions with Literature: Heuristics for the Exploration of Literary Texts." Chapter 3, "'But How Do You *Do* That?': Decision Making for the Seminar Facilitator," by Michael S. Hale and

Elizabeth A. City, provides a brief history and description of seminar instruction, then identifies four fulcrums (or key factors) that discussion facilitators should keep in mind when leading discussions. These are the safety of the participants, authentic participation, challenge, and ownership. The authors outline a prescription for enhancing the success of seminar discussions and include narrative accounts of actual discussions in their classes to illustrate decisions they make.

We think Chapter 4, "Implementing Whole-Class Literature Discussions: An Overview of the Teacher's Roles," will be especially helpful for teachers who are struggling to find their proper role in leading whole-class discussions. Sharon Eddleston and Raymond A. Philippot define five possible teacher roles (such as "facilitator" or "promoter of diverse perspectives") and provide practical tips for selecting texts, finding related writing activities, and creating supportive assessment strategies. In Chapter 5, "Whose Inquiry Is It Anyway? Using Students' Questions in the Teaching of Literature," G. Douglas Meyers describes ten different strategies for getting students to generate discussion questions. These include strategies such as creating one key question about a literary work; creating a list of important questions about a literary work and then rank-ordering these questions; creating a set of questions focused on literary elements; and creating a set of questions based on the questioning circle. This is another good chapter for those who want to give students a role in creating discussion questions.

Next, coeditor John S. Schmit's chapter, "Different Questions, Bigger Answers: Matching the Scope of Inquiry to Students' Needs," tells how one can use both closed-ended and open-ended questions to lead discussions. Using Ralph Ellison's "Battle Royal" (from *Invisible Man*) as a sample text, Schmit shows how teachers can use closed-ended questions to focus students' attention on a set of textual facts, to ensure that students understand an issue or idea, and to provide background for the upcoming open-ended questions. Then he shows how to use open-ended questions to facilitate a more comprehensive exploration of a text. Included in the chapter are sample closed-ended and open-ended questions for discussing "Battle Royal."

Mark Ensrud's chapter goes a step further, for in "Getting at What They Want to Know: Using Students' Questions to Direct Class Discussion" he outlines a strategy for getting high school students to create questions so they can lead their own discussions in small groups assigned by the teacher. In this variation of the Paideia seminar, Ensrud scaffolds his approach by first leading a large-group seminar on a story or poem, giving students practice in writing the four types of questions for a story they are reading (opening, closed-ended, open-ended, and core), using these questions for a second whole-class seminar led by the teacher, then having them write questions for another story. After the students write these questions, they are assigned to groups of eight to ten, and one student from each group is chosen to lead the discussion. Ensrud provides how-to-do-it information on such things as rules for a seminar, samples of the four types of questions, and a five-day schedule for implementing the model. Constructivist teachers will find this strategy right up their alley.

The book's second section, Strategies for Structuring Inquiry-Based Classrooms, includes five chapters. While these pieces provide specific ideas for daily activities, they focus more on how one might reorganize or change a language arts curriculum in order to implement an inquiry approach to teaching literature. Chapter 8, Elfie Israel's "Examining Multiple Perspectives in Literature," will be especially helpful for those who wish to use Socratic seminars, for it takes the reader through the steps needed to plan, execute, and assess seminars. Israel, a high school English teacher in Florida, shows how one can use Socratic seminars to discuss a variety of texts, and even musical compositions, films, and works of art. In a lively, personal voice, she talks about how she has led discussions on texts ranging from the Biblical story of Noah and the Ark, to Kate Chopin's novel *The Awakening,* to poems such as W. H. Auden's "Musee des Beaux Arts," to plays such as Euripides' *Medea,* to nonfiction texts such as John Hersey's *Hiroshima.* She also anticipates questions readers might have: How long should the seminar last? How do you assess student participation? How do you get reluctant students to participate? How do you select the text? Most important, she includes examples of questions to use for each text and lists some good beginning and closing questions teachers might ask.

Chapter 9, another by coeditor John S. Schmit, looks at ways in which classroom inquiry has changed and discusses the match between seminar or discussion questions and critical thinking models (particularly Bloom's Taxonomy). Titled "Practicing Critical Thinking through Inquiry into Literature," it talks about the need to teach students how to be prepared to answer questions. To ensure this preparation, teachers must construct a framework for questioning, one that moves students from content issues to interpretive issues. Here's where Bloom's Taxonomy comes in, for if the teacher moves questioning from knowledge to comprehension to application and then to the higher levels, he or she helps students become critical readers. Using a Socratic model,

Schmit shows how one can apply the levels of the taxonomy in preparing questions for three phases of discussion: exploration or discovery, careful examination of ideas, and extending the discussion outward. For those who seek a better way to incorporate Bloom's Taxonomy into an inquiry model for discussion, this chapter will be most helpful. Chapter 10, Martha Strom Cosgrove's "Moral Development and Meaning in Literature: A New Approach to Inquiry," focuses on how she and her colleagues in a Minnesota high school drew on Lawrence Kohlberg's theory of moral development to construct their curriculum. After introducing Kohlberg's model in one class period—discussing each stage with students—the teachers then selected readings related to each of the six stages: for example, Dinesen's "The Pearls" for stages one and two, Pericles' "Funeral Oration" for stages three and four, and *The Tempest* for stages five and six. This chapter would be useful for those seeking something other than a chronological or historical approach to organizing the teaching of literature. Beyond this, however, the author includes specific questions one can ask to address the issues/ideas raised in each phase of Kohlberg's model.

In the next chapter, Richard Beach takes us on a journey into the social worlds portrayed in literature ("Critical Inquiry Strategies for Responding to Social Worlds Portrayed in Literature") in hopes that doing so will enable students to make real-world connections to the literature they read. To assist the reader, he puts forth a model of inquiry which identifies critical strategies used in constructing components of these social worlds. He then illustrates the application of the model as it is used with middle school and high school students. Chapter 12, Jacqueline S. Thursby's "Inquiry, Folkloristics, and Discussion: Unbinding Literature in the Classroom," features a unique focus. Thursby invites students to explicate texts by looking at elements of folklore such as oral, material, customary, and belief lore. Teachers who are looking for "how-to-do-it" ideas will find her examples of folklore from two frequently taught texts (Harper Lee's *To Kill a Mockingbird* and Chaim Potok's *The Chosen*) to be helpful in understanding how her model works.

The final section of the book, Strategies for Assessing Inquiry-Based Approaches, includes two chapters on the topic of assessment. In Chapter 13, "Learning to Listen: Assessing Talk about Literature," Barbara G. Pace and Jane S. Townsend examine the kinds of questions that high school English teachers might ask about class discussions and the kinds of information they might collect. Then they provide a chart to illustrate how teachers might evaluate the process of a discussion. The final chapter, by Burt Plumb and John N. Ludy ("Seminars and Self-Assessment"), describes a method for assessing student performance in Socratic seminars and for performing pre- and post-course assessments. The emphasis is on self-assessment, and the forms used are included in the article.

We have also included an annotated bibliography of some of the most important books which inform our topic (see "Appendix: Suggestions for Further Reading"). We're confident that you will discover some good ideas for teaching from our book, but we also believe that these articles will open your eyes to new possibilities. If these predictions are on the money, or if you have some criticisms to offer or questions to ask, we would like to hear from you. You can e-mail us at holdenjn@ earthlink.net or schmit@augsburg.edu.

Works Cited

Auciello, Joseph. "Chronicle of a Battle Foretold: Curriculum and Social Change." *English Journal* 89.4 (2000): 89–96.

Beach, Richard, and Jamie Myers. *Inquiry-Based English Instruction: Engaging Students in Life and Literature*. New York: Teachers College P, 2001.

Bloom, Benjamin S. *Taxonomy of Educational Objectives: The Classification of Educational Goals. Handbook 1: Cognitive Domain*. New York: McKay, 1956.

Friedman, Audrey A. "Nurturing Reflective Judgment through Literature-Based Inquiry." *English Journal* 89.6 (2000): 96–104.

"Inquiry." Def. 1, 2, 3. *The American Heritage Dictionary of the English Language*. 1969.

"13 Principles of Best Practice." *Arts Education: Research, Assessment & Curriculum* 4.1 (Winter 2000): 1–6. (Published by the Perpich Center for Arts Education in Golden Valley, MN.)

Zemelman, Steven, Harvey Daniels, and Arthur Hyde. *Best Practice: New Standards for Teaching and Learning in America's Schools*. 2nd ed. Portsmouth, NH: Heinemann, 1998.

Acknowledgments

Our interest in teaching students to inquire into literary texts began with our participation in workshops on constructing Socratic seminars. In addition, our study of constructivist theories of learning shaped the ideas contained in this book. We also share a philosophical belief in the need for democratic classrooms, ones in which students are not only encouraged but taught how to build their own interpretations of literature.

Visits to Sullivan High School in Chicago and Monroe Community School in St. Paul, Minnesota, convinced us that students of all backgrounds and abilities were capable of developing sophisticated, thoughtful ideas when their teachers provided the right sort of classroom. We wish to thank the teachers and administrators of these schools for sharing their classrooms with us.

We owe debts to a number of people who were influential in the development of our own Socratic classroom practices and whose ideas are reflected in these pages: John Clark, Gene Galatowitsch, Rita Kaplan, Anne Kaufman, Marie McNeff, Michael Strong, Elaine Sutton, and Patricia Weiss. We also owe a debt to all of our wonderful English teacher colleagues who have struggled (as we have) to share their love of literature by discussing it with students. While they were not at all times successful, they always brought into the classroom their passion for the life-changing words of story.

To those institutions and offices that supported this work we are also grateful: the Centers for Professional Development at Augsburg and St. Olaf Colleges, the English department at Augsburg, the education and English departments at St. Olaf, and the Paideia Group, Inc.

We appreciate the clear guidance and support we have received from the editorial staff at the National Council of Teachers of English as well, especially that of Peter Feely and Tom Tiller.

Finally, we wish to express our gratitude to our families for their patience, support, and assistance in the completion of this project: Deborah Appleman, Kelly Bunte, Caroline Holden, Chris Holden, Heather Holden Larson, and Dwight Larson.

1 Socratic Seminars and Inquiry Teaching—An Overview

James Holden
St. Olaf College

In the beginning was Socrates, the first Adam who begat John Dewey who begat Lev Vygotsky who begat Jean Piaget who begat Paolo Freire who begat Mortimer Adler. Along with Louise Rosenblatt and a number of other contemporary theorists, these are just several of the most recent in a long line of "descendants" of the great teacher Socrates, who, tramping along the dusty streets of Athens some twenty-four hundred years ago, coaxed his followers along by asking thoughtful questions in order to help them discover truth. By persistent further questioning, a method revealed in Plato's *Dialogues*, Socrates became the midwife who "help[ed] participants give birth to their own ideas and insights" (Swenson 3). He termed this notion of giving birth to ideas "maieutics," and the labor which produced these ideas was the dialectic or conversational method.

One example may serve to illustrate. In a dialogue with Menon, Socrates attempts to prove to Menon that "there is no such thing as teaching, only remembering" (qtd. in Warmington and Rouse 42). He asks a young boy a series of questions about geometric spaces and lines in order to bring knowledge out of him. Here in Socrates' own words is the essence of the method: "Look out if you find me teaching and explaining to him, instead of asking for his opinions" (48). This asking-for-one's-opinions as practiced by Socrates in the fifth century B.C.E. is what has come to be called the Socratic method, a method that has evolved into the Socratic seminar with its focus on discussions of ideas based on a common text. One can also see how this Socratic method has influenced English teachers who employ inquiry techniques in leading discussions of literature.

What follows in this chapter is a brief historical overview of these important nineteenth- and twentieth-century descendants of Socrates, a description of one type of Socratic seminar (the Paideia seminar) and how it is being used in K–12 school settings, comments about Socratic seminars being used in college settings, and some observations about Socratic seminars and constructivist learning theories. The chapter concludes with remarks about current books on inquiry approaches to teaching literature and descriptions of some classroom models that are currently being used.

Descendants of Socrates

The first descendant of Socrates noted here is John Dewey, arguably the most influential educator in United States history. In "My Pedagogic Creed," Dewey states his belief that education is mainly a social process, that "the school is primarily a social institution" (22), and that the child's social activities should be the focus of all school subjects. Constructing knowledge for Dewey was therefore accomplished in a community "through language as a mediating tool for learning" and by collaborating "with their [i.e., students'] own and others' thoughts and feelings" (qtd. in Hirtle 91). For Dewey, the typical schoolroom of his day, with its desks organized in straight rows and bolted to the floor, was not conducive to learning in a social setting. In the second of his 1899 "School and Society" lectures, he faults the old education for "its passivity of attitude, its mechanical massing of children, its uniformity of curriculum and method," and for locating the "center of gravity outside the child" (Dewey 53). In this traditional model, still common all over the world, the locus is in the teacher and the textbook. Dewey suggests that a better model might be that of the ideal home and family, where

> we find the child learning through the social converse and constitution of the family. There are certain points of interest and value to him in the conversation carried on: statements are made, inquiries arise, topics are discussed, and the child continually learns. He states his experiences, his misconceptions are corrected. (53)

Indeed, learning takes place in this setting much in the same way it took place when Socrates engaged his compatriots in dialogue, only here the questioners could be both parents and children. Such a model, Dewey maintains, might be applied to an ideal school, which, like the ideal home, "would have a miniature laboratory in which his [the child's] inquiries could be directed" (53).

Another descendant of Socrates is Lev Vygotsky, a Russian educator and psychologist who believed that "speech is the first tool that culture provides for the child to engage in collaborative thinking with others, through talk that accompanies, directs, and, reflects the problem solving required in everyday social activity" (qtd. in Hirtle 91). Vygotsky, as Dixon-Krauss observes, thought the behaviorists' view of development was too reliant on the individual's passive responses to the environment. Rather, Vygotsky "found his explanation of consciousness in *socially meaningful activity*; that is, we know ourselves because of our interactions with others" (9).

After we interact with others in a social context, we then develop intellectually by thinking about what we have learned and internalizing this knowledge. In order then to help students learn at their "zone of proximal development" (the area between a child's present functioning on his or her own and the child's potential performance level with assistance), "the teacher mediates or augments the child's ability to perform various tasks by providing guidance and support primarily though social dialogue" (Dixon-Krauss 15). The context for this support, either from a teacher or the child's peers, is more often than not a collaborative group setting such as literature study groups, learning teams, or discussion groups. This collaborative group setting is precisely the model employed in the Socratic seminar and in other programs such as Literature Circles or Questioning Circles. One can imagine Vygotsky being pleased that his beliefs would be implemented in ways such as these.

Next in line is Jean Piaget, the Swiss psychologist who has given us a paradigm for how the minds of children develop. Piaget, another proponent of dialogue as a way to learn, speaks about the importance of social interaction and the activity of the learner in cognitive development. In *Piaget for the Classroom Teacher*, Wadsworth cites Piaget's belief that peer interaction is necessary in order to break down the child's egocentric thinking and to validate his or her views of reality (107). Socialization thus plays a major role in helping children organize and communicate their thoughts, and this is very much an active process of learning. Constance Kamii expands on this view:

> In summary, the pedagogical implications of Piaget's theory suggest the kind of reform that makes learning truly active and encourages social interactions among pupils to cultivate a critical spirit. . . . The emphasis of a Piagetian school is definitely on the child's own thinking and judgment, rather than on the use of correct language and adult logic. (213–14)

It does not require an intellectual leap to see the connection between such a model and the tactics employed by Socrates centuries ago. The level of discourse will likely be on a higher plane at the learning stage Piaget calls formal operations (11–15 years) than at the preoperational stage (2–7 years), but this active social discourse is possible at all levels of development.

One late-twentieth-century descendant of Socrates is the influential Brazilian educator and author Paolo Freire, who also recognized the importance of dialogue in learning. For Freire, working as he did with illiterate peasants who lacked a voice, "becoming literate was an act of taking control, of exercising power . . . 'conscientizacao,' sometimes translated 'conscientization' or 'consciousness raising'" (qtd. in Smith and Smith 429). It is very much akin to Socrates' notion of giving birth to ideas and is what Freire called going from a "'culture of silence' to finding one's voice" (429). The teacher helps learners "assume the role of knowing subject in dialogue with the educator" (Hirtle 92). As Parkay and Stanford observe, "Freire stressed the significance of dialogue in his pedagogy and contrasted it with the traditional teacher-student relationship . . . in which teachers deposit their expertise into empty accounts" (147).

Yet another descendant of Socrates is Mortimer Adler, cofounder of the Great Books Foundation program and an important twentieth-century educational philosopher. Adler and his associates, in their 1984 book *The Paideia Program*, described a Socratic method they called the Paideia seminar. This method, according to Adler, consists of three modes of teaching: the "didactic" (or lecture) mode employed by the Sophists of Socrates' time, the "coaching" mode, and the "seminar" mode. The Paideia seminar, according to Adler, is a conversation that focuses on books or other products of human art. "If books, they must be books that present ideas or broach issues, not books that are catalogues of information or direct expositions of factual knowledge" (16). This conversation is a joint search, moderated by a leader, in which ideas in a text are clarified and in which something new and unexpected is discovered, a discussion in which both the teacher/moderator and students sit so that they can face one another as they talk. Adler, paying homage to Socrates, says, "Questioning students about something they have read so as to help them improve their understanding of basic ideas and values is a procedure that can appropriately be called Socratic" (15–16).

One Type of Socratic Seminar

Since the publication of *The Paideia Program* and its call for a one-track system of schooling to meet the needs of a politically classless society, over seventy-five schools have implemented Paideia seminar programs into their curricula. In one Paideia school, Sullivan High School in Chicago, students develop critical thinking skills by reading original source materials and discussing them in a structured Socratic seminar format. "Seminars are offered on a regular basis in English, history, math, and science classes; monthly as a voluntary enrichment activity; and four times yearly as a special event in which the entire school participates" (*Sullivan High School Handbook* 4). For example, during the 1996–97 school year, the four all-school seminars were based on the following readings: "No Name Woman" by Maxine Hong Kingston, "Influence of Democracy on the Family" by Tocqueville, "Everyday Use" by Alice Walker, and a speech by Harvey Milk entitled "A City of Neighborhoods." And every year the Paideia Group, Inc., located in Chapel Hill, North Carolina, sponsors regional workshops and a national conference in Chicago for teachers who wish to learn how to lead seminars.

Socratic Seminars in College Settings

In addition to the many K–12 schools which employ Paideia seminars, some colleges have adopted a Socratic seminar format. The first of these Socratic programs in the United States was instituted at St. John's College in Annapolis, Maryland, in 1937. Scott Buchanan, the architect of St. John's College, coined the term Socratic seminars "to refer to the Socratic discussion classes instituted with the New program" (Strong 5). To this day the Socratic seminar is the mode of teaching at St. John's and its sister institution located in Santa Fe, New Mexico. One Midwestern college using a Socratic format is Luther College in Decorah, Iowa, where all first-year students participate in the Paideia I course called "The Common First-Year Prologue to the Liberal Arts," taught by the departments of history and English. First-year students receive four credits in history and four in English in a course designed to develop "critical reading and writing skills as students read significant historical and literary texts, listen to lectures, write essays, and participate in class discussions and confer with other students and the instructor" (*The Paideia I Reader* 5). The text/syllabus is designed by the Paideia I faculty and includes a first semester unit on classical Greece and another on the sixteenth-century in Europe; the second semester adds a study of non-Western culture (a unit on China) and includes a unit on American diversity and nationhood (with a study of the Norwegian American and African American experiences). Throughout both semesters, professors deliver lectures (the didactic mode of teaching) on a text or topic and follow up with a Paideia seminar the next day.

Socratic Seminars and Constructivist Learning

While most seminars in all of these aforementioned settings are planned and led by adults, there are some high school and college teachers who have trained students to lead their own Socratic seminars (see the chapter in this book by Mark Ensrud). These teachers have embraced constructivist points of view, assuming that learners construct their own understandings of the world in which they live and that "teachers want students to take responsibility for their own learning, to be autonomous thinkers, to . . . pose—and seek to answer—important questions" (Brooks and Brooks 13).

From my own experience in teaching students to prepare and lead seminars at Gustavus Adolphus and St. Olaf Colleges (in both education and first-year writing classes), I am persuaded that giving students a chance to plan and lead seminars connects very well with current constructivist notions of how people learn. For instance, during the 1991–92 school year, I surveyed fifty students to find out how they felt about the five small-group seminars they participated in. Using a Likert-style survey to assess the success of the program, I found the students to be enthusiastic about leading and participating in their own seminars: 89 percent liked the student-led seminar concept, 91 percent felt that seminars gave students a better opportunity to participate in discussions than they had in large-group settings, 83 percent said that the seminar leaders were good at guiding participants and asking important open-ended questions, 68 percent said they learned something new, and 89 percent thought we should repeat the seminar program the next semester (Holden 24).

Constructivists hold the view that we must take responsibility for our own learning, and, therefore, that "the teacher's responsibility is to create educational environments that permit students to assume the responsibility that is rightfully and naturally theirs" (Brooks and Brooks 49). It is in fact not so important what the teacher does but "what the teacher gets the child to do" (Brandt 11). Teachers must therefore create opportunities for inquiry, providing challenging and appropriate materials for learning, and facilitating teacher-to-student and student-to-student interactions.

Inside constructivist classrooms, one will observe teachers attempting to connect learning to the world outside the classroom, assessing through observations of students at work and through student exhibitions and portfolios, seeking students' points of view and listening to them, using cooperative learning strategies, encouraging students to talk to one another, letting students do the work. In such classrooms, "thought flourishes as questions are asked, not as answers are found" (Frank Smith 129).

It seems to me that the Socratic seminar and the Paideia seminar are close siblings, for in both there is a community of learners who share ideas by reading, listening, talking, thinking, and supporting one another. In both, the students become responsible actors, and in both there are obvious connections to constructivist learning theories. For example, in constructivist classrooms and in Paideia or Socratic seminars, student questions are valued, there is a reliance on primary sources of data, students are seen as intelligent thinkers with emerging theories about the world, students work in groups where cooperation is valued, risk taking is encouraged, the teacher mediates and facilitates, and students take responsibility for their own learning (Brooks and Brooks 17).

Rosenblatt and Books on Inquiry Approaches

For those of us who are literature teachers, perhaps the name that comes to mind most often is Louise Rosenblatt, another descendant of Socrates. Rosenblatt, in her enormously influential *Literature as Exploration,* advanced the notion that reading literature, far from being a passive process, is an intense personal activity in which the student "raises personally meaningful questions" (viii). To some extent, her book was a reaction against the prevailing theory of New Criticism which emphasized correct interpretations of a text, but it was mainly an attempt to help readers "discover the satisfactions of literature" and to assist them in evoking "meaning from the text by leading [them] to reflect self-critically on this process" (26). Certainly Dewey, Piaget, Vygotsky, and constructivist learning theorists have been important in moving teachers to consider inquiry approaches discussed later in this chapter, but one also thinks of the seminal work on cooperative learning done by brothers David and Roger Johnson of the University of Minnesota, particularly in their 1975 book *Learning Together and Alone.* And the work of Robert Probst on reader-response theory (see his *Response and Analysis: Teaching Literature in Junior and Senior High School*) figures prominently in any discussion of inquiry teaching. One of our contributors, Richard Beach, has also written a book which follows on the heels of Probst *(A Teacher's Introduction to Reader-Response Theories),* and Jeffrey Wilhelm's work (particularly *"You Gotta BE the Book": Teaching Engaged and Reflective Reading with Adolescents*) is especially worth noting.

Others who have advocated inquiry approaches include Judith Langer (*Envisioning Literature: Literary Understanding and Literature Instruction* and, as editor, *Literature Instruction: A Focus on Student Response*); Susan Hynds (*On the Brink: Negotiating Literature and Life With Adolescents*); Jeffrey Golub (*Activities for an Interactive Classroom* and, as coeditor with Louann Reid, *Reflective Activities: Helping Students Connect with Texts*); Peter Smagorinsky, Tom McCann, and Stephen Kern (*Explorations: Introductory Activities for Literature and Composition, 7–12*); Michael W. Smith (*Understanding Unreliable Narrators: Reading between the Lines in the Literature Classroom*); and Peter J. Rabinowitz (*Authorizing Readers: Resistance and Respect in the Teaching of Literature*, with Michael W. Smith). I am also reminded of a book I have used in my education classes, *Open to Question: The Art of Teaching and Learning by Inquiry* (by Walter L. Bateman); and a book such as *Getting Started with Literature Circles*, by Katherine L. Schlick Noe and Nancy J. Johnson, would be helpful for those who wish to incorporate this technique into their middle school or elementary language arts classes.

Two recent books approach inquiry learning from quite different, even unique, viewpoints. One is Deborah Appleman's *Critical Encounters in High School English: Teaching Literary Theory to Adolescents*. Assuming that texts may very well have multiple meanings, Appleman teaches students to examine texts by using the lenses of literary theory, such as reader-response, Marxist, feminist, and deconstructionist approaches. Such close readings, Appleman posits, "will encourage young people to develop the intellectual flexibility they need to read not only literary texts but the cultural texts that surround and often confuse them" (xiii). The other new book, written by Richard Beach and Jamie Myers, is called *Inquiry-Based English Instruction: Engaging Students in Life and Literature*. Beach and Myers propose that teachers ask students to focus on how social worlds are constructed when they read a text; that is, how these worlds are constructed, negotiated, maintained, and contested through literacy, language, media, and all forms of symbolic interaction.

I know I am forgetting other important books, and there are many fine individual essays about this topic as well. For example, see Audrey A. Friedman's *English Journal* article titled "Nurturing Reflective Judgment through Literature-Based Inquiry" or Melvyn J. Haber's chapter "Using Student Questions to Promote Active Reading and Participation" in *Activating the Passive Student* (Stanford et al.). (For more information about selected titles mentioned in this text, see the annotated bibliography, Suggestions for Further Reading, at the end of the book.)

Some Classroom Inquiry Models

Inquiry strategies are being used in English classrooms all over this country against a public caterwauling for a return to the basics (whatever that is or was), more standardized testing, more school choice, and more old-fashioned phonics so Johnny can once again read. Perhaps the most well-known inquiry strategy is reader-response theory, a method that encourages multiple and even contradictory perspectives on a text. Another approach, Literature Circles, also encourages inquiry by giving students a chance to choose their own reading materials, to discuss their own questions, and to share ideas about a book. A third model is that of the Touchstones Program, which employs short, unfamiliar texts to force students, gathered together in what is called a "discourse community," to work out together their reasoning about enduring themes and issues ("Toward a Community of Learners" 2). A number of schools use this program in order to hone students' thinking skills, to get them to express themselves orally, to listen, to use evidence to support an opinion. Also, Christenbury and Kelly have developed a model they call Questioning Circles, which focuses on questions about the reader, questions about the text, and questions about the world.

All this groundwork which has been laid out for us, beginning with Socrates and his persistent method of questioning, has led us to this new day, a day in which we are moving away from the model of the central authority over meaning (the teacher as Supreme Intelligence) to that of the student as meaning-maker and meaning-discoverer.

Works Cited

Adler, Mortimer J., ed. *The Paideia Program: An Educational Syllabus.* New York: Macmillan, 1984.

Appleman, Deborah. *Critical Encounters in High School English: Teaching Literary Theory to Adolescents.* New York: Teachers College P, and Urbana, IL: NCTE, 2000.

Bateman, Walter L. *Open to Question: The Art of Teaching and Learning by Inquiry.* San Francisco: Jossey-Bass, 1990.

Beach, Richard. *A Teacher's Introduction to Reader-Response Theories.* Urbana, IL: NCTE, 1993.

Beach, Richard, and Jamie Myers. *Inquiry-Based English Instruction: Engaging Students in Life and Literature.* New York: Teachers College P, 2001.

Brandt, Ron. "On Restructuring Roles and Relationships: A Conversation with Phil Schlechty." *Educational Leadership* 51.2 (1993): 8–11.

Brooks, Jacqueline Grennon, and Martin G. Brooks. *In Search of Understanding: The Case for Constructivist Classrooms.* Alexandria, VA: Association for Supervision and Curriculum Development, 1993.

Christenbury, Leila, and Patricia P. Kelly. *Questioning: A Path to Critical Thinking.* Urbana, IL: ERIC Clearinghouse on Reading and Communication Skills and NCTE, 1983.

Dewey, John. *Dewey on Education: Selections.* Ed. Martin S. Dworkin. New York: Teachers College P, 1959.

Dixon-Krauss, Lisbeth. *Vygotsky in the Classroom: Mediated Literacy Instruction and Assessment.* White Plains, NY: Longman, 1996.

Friedman, Audrey A. "Nurturing Reflective Judgment through Literature-Based Inquiry." *English Journal* 89.6 (2000): 96–104.

Golub, Jeffrey N. *Activities for an Interactive Classroom.* Urbana, IL: NCTE, 1994.

Hirtle, Jeannine St. Pierre. "Social Constructivism (Coming to Terms)." *English Journal.* 85.1 (1996): 91–92.

Holden, James. "'Tis a Communication Devoutly to Be Wished': The Paideia Seminar in Teacher Education Classes." *Mankato Statement* (Spring 1993): 19–26.

Hynds, Susan. *On the Brink: Negotiating Literature and Life with Adolescents.* New York: Teachers College P, 1997.

Johnson, David W., and Johnson, Roger T. *Learning Together and Alone: Cooperation, Competition, and Individualization.* Englewood Cliffs, NJ: Prentice-Hall, 1975.

Kamii, Constance. "Pedagogical Principles Derived from Piaget's Theory: Relevance for Educational Practice." *Piaget in the Classroom.* Ed. Milton Schwebel and Jane Raph. New York: Basic, 1973. 199–215.

Langer, Judith A. *Envisioning Literature: Literary Understanding and Literature Instruction.* New York: Teachers College P, 1995.

———, ed. *Literature Instruction: A Focus on Student Response.* Urbana, IL: NCTE, 1992.

Noe, Katherine L. Schlick, and Nancy J. Johnson. *Getting Started with Literature Circles.* Norwood, MA: Christopher-Gordon, 1999.

The Paideia I Reader. Decorah, IA: Luther College, 1994.

Parkay, Forrest W., and Beverly Hardcastle Stanford. *Becoming a Teacher.* 4th ed. Boston: Allyn and Bacon, 1998.

Probst, Robert E. *Response and Analysis: Teaching Literature in Junior and Senior High School.* Portsmouth, NH: Boynton/Cook, 1988.

Rabinowitz, Peter J., and Michael W. Smith. *Authorizing Readers: Resistance and Respect in the Teaching of Literature.* New York: Teachers College P, 1998.

Reid, Louann, and Jeffrey N. Golub, eds. *Reflective Activities: Helping Students Connect with Texts.* Urbana, IL: NCTE, 1998.

Rosenblatt, Louise M. *Literature as Exploration.* New York: Noble and Noble, 1968.

Smagorinsky, Peter, Tom McCann, and Stephen Kern. *Explorations: Introductory Activities for Literature and Composition, 7–12.* Urbana, IL: ERIC Clearinghouse on Reading and Communication Skills and NCTE, 1987.

Smith, Frank. *To Think.* New York: Teachers College P, 1990.

Smith, L. Glenn, and Joan K. Smith. *Lives in Education: A Narrative of People and Ideas.* New York: St. Martin's, 1994.

Smith, Michael W. *Understanding Unreliable Narrators: Reading between the Lines in the Literature Classroom.* Urbana, IL: NCTE, 1991.

Stanford, Gene, Chair, and the Committee on Classroom Practices, eds. *Activating the Passive Student.* Urbana, IL: NCTE, 1978.

Strong, Michael. *The Habit of Thought: From Socratic Seminars to Socratic Practice.* Chapel Hill, NC: New View, 1997.

Sullivan High School Handbook. Bellingham, WA: Premier School Agendas, 1996.

Swenson, William. "Torpedo Fish, Gadfly, Midwife." *Paideia Partners* (Spring 1991): 1–4.

"Toward a Community of Learners." Far West Laboratory for Educational Research and Development. No Date: 1–2

Wadsworth, Barry J. *Piaget for the Classroom Teacher.* New York: Longman, 1978.

Warmington, Eric H., and Philip G. Rouse, eds. *Great Dialogues.* By Plato. Trans. W. H. D. Rouse. New York: New American, 1956.

Wilhelm, Jeffrey D. *"You Gotta BE the Book": Teaching Engaged and Reflective Reading with Adolescents.* New York: Teachers College P, 1997.

Part I Strategies for Inquiring into Texts

2 Master Questions and the Teaching of Literature

Mark Gellis
Kettering University

This article outlines a student-centered approach for teaching literature to students who are not English majors. The approach emphasizes active learning, moving away from an approach built around lectures given by an instructor. Instead, the emphasis is on giving students a framework for critical exploration and encouraging them to develop their skills as critical readers, not only with traditional essay assignments but also with reaction essays and extensive in-class writing. The approach was designed, in particular, for students with limited expertise and experience in literary criticism who might also have limited motivation or confidence in their abilities to study literature. It draws in part on the work done by David Bartholomae and Anthony Petrosky, but also on research in active learning. Because the approach focuses on asking questions rather than providing students with information, and incorporates exploring both personal reactions to literature and objective analyses of the texts being studied, it is also portable; it can be used to examine any kind of literature. For these reasons, I believe this approach may prove useful at various educational levels, ranging from secondary schools and community colleges to introductory courses at four-year colleges.

In all of these circumstances, students are usually novices, and novices in at least two ways. They are not only learning about the literature itself but are also learning about how literature is discussed. In our English classes, students enter the ongoing conversations about literature and, as a result, must learn the conventions of our discourse communities, conventions about what kind of people have the right to speak, and what kinds of discussion are accepted. Students are learning which topics are "good" topics, what kind of supporting material is appropriate for these essays, which sources can be used to back up their arguments, and which styles of writing their teachers find acceptable. At some levels we are trying to prepare our students for college-level writing; at others, we are trying to prepare them for graduate school. In both cases, however, it is in these classes that our students learn the Standard English of English.

Helping students make this transition can be facilitated with heuristics (an exploratory strategy for generating knowledge). Exploratory heuristics are now commonly used in composition classes but seem to be less popular in literature classes. The reasons for this difference are unclear, but it may be that literature instructors consider these heuristics to be ineffective. My own experience, however, is that certain "master questions" can be applied to a wide range of literary works. Furthermore, I have found that an effective alternative to lectures is to use a "write-talk" approach in a literature class. Students will be given one "master question" to write on for about ten minutes in relation to the literary work being discussed, and then the class will discuss the answers that various students have provided.

The advantages of this approach are numerous. First, and most important, this approach can transform a class from a teacher-centered lecture into a student-centered discussion. Instructors still have to guide the discussion and will probably speak more often than any individual student, but students will do far more thinking and talking than they would if they were simply taking notes on a lecture. The second advantage is that unlike some other traditional forms of discussion-based classes, almost all students can contribute significantly to the discussion. In any class there will usually be a few students who like literature, have good ideas and questions, and like talking in class. It is very easy to fall into the trap of turning the class into a conversation between the instructor and these students, leaving the rest to passively watch the show. With the write-talk method, students are not asked to come up with answers on the spot; they are given several minutes to think about their answers and to write them down (so they cannot forget what they have come up with). Thus, an instructor can rely on a wider range of students for answers. Often, when those students who need a little more time to think are given that time, they come up with original and interesting ideas. Finally, it is quite likely that giving students the opportunity to brainstorm and articulate their ideas about literature not only in a couple of long essays but also in twenty or thirty short writing assignments (which should not be graded, because they are exploratory exercises) will increase their understanding of particular works and their retention of those insights. Most of the work available on active learning (e.g., Bean, 1996; Bonwell and Eison, 1991; Stice, 1995) backs up these assumptions.

So what are these "master questions," and how do I use them? I use three approaches. First, I have developed a heuristic that students can use while they are reading the various assigned works. The heuristic, quite simply, is a large set of questions that are applicable to a wide range of works of literature, but especially to fiction, drama, and narrative poetry. It was not designed to be a comprehensive theory of literature but rather a tool kit for novice readers of literature, a set of entry points for their encounters with literature. The goal was simply to give them the means not only to explore literature but also to continue doing so with the books they would read and the films they would see once they had finished with us. With that spirit of pragmatism and play invoked, I refer to my system as "playing twenty questions with literature." The handout was originally a collection of notes and prompts I had written up for myself to guide class discussion, but my students asked me for copies so frequently that I placed it online at http://www.kettering.edu/~mgellis/HANDT015. HTM. (See also the appendix at the end of this chapter.)

The second set of "master questions" is used for a reaction essay that students must complete for each of the major readings. I ask students to write a simple one-page essay that answers the following three questions:

1. Did you like the text? Did you find it interesting, entertaining? Why or why not?

2. Regardless of whether you liked the text, what do you consider worth discussing? Which questions could we try to answer? What topics should be explored?

3. Regardless of whether you like the text, and regardless of which issues you think might be discussed, is the text literature? Why or why not?

The first question is deliberately designed to make engaging the text a personal matter. From the very beginning, students are able to announce their ownership of the text; they begin with an emotional rather than an intellectual response. And emotional ownership cannot be attacked— no one can argue that you do not really feel a certain way about something. If you are enlightened by a text, that is your experience; if you are repulsed by a text, that is also your experience. No one can say you are right or wrong to be delighted, disgusted, horrified, confused, bored, outraged, or brought to tears or laughter by a book or a poem. For example, if a student likes bad horror movies, the sort that involve hapless coeds stalked by disfigured lunatics, or animated tales involving mice with delusions of grandeur, it is not hard to prove that these films have little intellectual or aesthetic value (although they often have more than we suspect), but no one can prove that the student does not like them.

Ownership is, I think, a real issue. We own the texts we read. As Stanley Fish and others have pointed out, a text does not even exist in any meaningful way outside of a reader or a community of readers. (Ray Bradbury has a more poetic way of expressing this—he describes a scene he did not put in the original version of *Fahrenheit 451* in which one character "kills" books by owning them but never reading them.) While I want students to become engaged with the text in this way, I also want them to think about their reactions. It is not enough for them to tell me that they liked or hated a particular book. I ask them to explain their feelings, if they can, or at least to identify the sections or aspects of the text that made them feel the way they felt. Sometimes this leads directly into the second part of their reaction essays.

The second question, in which students list aspects of the text they think should be discussed, allows students to continue their ownership of both the text and the course. While the instructor will usually choose some of the topics that are going to be included in the discussion of a particular text, the students are also determining, as a class, what issues and questions should be among those discussed. In many cases, of course, the students choose topics and issues that the instructor would have chosen anyway; even here, however, students will feel as if they have an equal share in how the conversation develops. As with the way that people own their conversations outside of the classroom, this ownership of the course is likely to increase motivation and interest among students. An additional advantage is that students will sometimes identify aspects of the text that the instructor had not previously thought to examine.

The third question, in which students evaluate the text as literature, requires that they both create and defend a definition of literature and then argue for the quality of a text based on that definition. As such, it stimulates critical thinking and critical discussion on an issue that must be considered central to almost all examinations of the arts—what is art, anyway?

All this echoes what Alfred North Whitehead said regarding the mastery of a discipline. According to Whitehead, the three stages in mastery are romance, precision, and generalization. While there are obvious differences between the approach Whitehead recommends and the one I am discussing here, his three stages correspond roughly to the three questions I ask students to answer. The first question is "romantic" in the sense that it involves a personal, often emotional engagement with the text, a first impression followed by critical reflection. The second stage, precision, is matched by the second question's demand that students provide a detailed exposition of issues, characters, and so on that they believe should be discussed. Finally, the third stage, generalization, is similar to the third question, which asks students to make a critical judgment about the text that involves moving beyond it. In fact, Deanne Bogdan has discussed an approach to using Whitehead's stages of mastery as a way of teaching literature. More important, I think that my approach is animated by the same spirit as that of Robert Scholes, who argues in *Textual Power* that "our job is not to produce 'readings' for our students but to give them the tools for producing their own" (24).

The response essay, if used well, can be a remarkable tool for class discussion. All one needs to do is have students read (or summarize) their reaction essays—sharing and defending their ideas about a text to the class—to make the opening day of discussing any particular work of literature full of interesting and often insightful commentary. Having students write the essay means that they will (in theory, at least) have read the novel or play by the time one is ready to start discussing it. In addition, students have already had time to explore, articulate, and record their ideas. If they wish to speak in an impromptu manner, summarizing and extrapolating from their reaction essays, they may do so. If they simply wish to read the essay, because they do not have anything else to add at this point, they may do this as well. Best of all, they are not simply waiting passively for me to tell them what the work means. To complete this assignment they must engage the text actively, grapple with it, and figure out for themselves what it means.

Two quick tips about using the reaction essay. I allow students to revise the reaction essay while we are discussing the work; they only have to hand it in once we are finished discussing the novel or play in question. This way the essay not only serves as an exploratory device but also provides students with an option to "edit" their opinions, if they wish to do so. Sometimes students feel their initial views of a text are in error or that their essay is incomplete. In addition, I do not assign a letter grade for the reaction essays. Instead, I use an R, check (√), plus (+) system. An R grade means "Revise and Resubmit." It is used when a student simply has not done the assignment properly. There is no actual penalty, but the student will not get credit for the assignment until he or she has satisfactorily revised the paper. A check grade means the student has done acceptable work. It will neither raise nor lower the grade determined by the student's work on longer papers, exams, and speeches, but instead means that the student has completed that part of the required work for the course. A plus mark, however, means that the reaction essay is of unusual quality (an "A"). I generally raise the student's overall grade by one percent for each plus received on the five or six reaction essays written in a term. In this manner the reaction essays serve as "required extra credit." The assignments cannot harm students, since the worst that can happen is that they may have to revise a poorly written essay, but these assignments have the potential to earn students several additional points for their grades. I believe this removes pressure from the students, which may encourage them to explore and experiment.

The third set of "master questions" are the ones I use for my "write-talk" approach. What questions should a teacher ask? Frankly, I think the only real answer to this question is "Whatever the teacher thinks is a good question." While a list of questions could be developed by committee to use in all common sections of a course, writing their own questions allows teachers to bring their own special interests and strengths into the classroom.

As examples, I find the following ideas or themes both interesting and useful: the nature of heroism, the nature of evil, and the relationships between individuals and society and between men and women. I also think looking at literature as rhetoric, as argument in the form of fable, and treating a text as a way for an author to infect an audience with his or her ideas, are central to understanding literature. So these are some of the ideas or themes I use when creating "master questions" to initiate class discussions. Someone else, however, might choose completely different ideas or themes.

In short, what I try to do as often as possible is to replace the traditional lecture-discussion approach with one in which students do most of the talking. This is actually easier than it sounds. Once we have spent a day or two reading and discussing reaction essays, I begin the class by providing the students with a prompt, usually one adapted from the issues they have identified in their initial reaction essays. Students spend about ten minutes writing a response; then they read and discuss the short responses they have written. In small classes this means that every student gets an opportunity to contribute during each class meeting. It also means that the class discussion is not dominated by the instructor and two or three bright and/or outspoken students. In larger classes, of course, it is important not to rely only on these more articulate students. Some students, particularly those who are shy about speaking in public, can be left out of the discussion unless the teacher actively encourages their involvement.

Using this technique means that students spend far more time talking than listening. It avoids the problem of students not being ready for a question by giving them time to think through their answers and then record those answers so they do not forget them. I also encourage students to maintain a journal where they can keep and then add to their reaction essays and in-class responses. (Both Douglas M. Tedards and Carl R. Lovitt have discussed in detail the use of journals in literature classes.) An interesting effect is that, on occasion, students will stop talking to me about the text and instead start talking with each other, replacing a teacher-student dynamic with a student-student one. This suggests that, at least for a few minutes, I have helped transform these students from isolated and passive listeners into an interacting community of active thinkers. One final advantage is that this approach also gives students practice in public speaking.

To sum up, I believe this approach allows students who are not English majors, and who have perhaps had difficult or even traumatic experiences with reading and writing, to take some control over the critical process of reading a text. Along with Pianko, I believe this sense of being authorized, this sense of ownership, will not only motivate students but also improve the quality of their writing. I believe students who see themselves as authorized explorers of the text write with more confidence and more interest than those who see themselves as powerless, as unconnected, perhaps even as being punished with literature or being shown how stupid they must be because they do not see what the teacher sees. I confess I am not aware of any empirical studies that would scientifically prove this last claim. Although there is quite a bit of research available on writing anxiety, there does not seem to be much on "reading anxiety." I believe, however, that this could prove a fruitful avenue for empirical research in the teaching of English, possibly by comparing both performance and attitudes before and after students take a class like the one described in this article. Kirsch and Sullivan, as well as Lauer and Asher, have discussed methods of empirical research as applied to composition classes; these methods could be easily adapted to studying the effectiveness of teaching in literature classes.

To conclude, I believe I have developed a method for teaching literature that could be used anywhere, but which will prove especially useful when working with students who are still beginning their initiation into the humanities. For these students, and I think for others, too, my approach can be effective, productive, and enjoyable for both instructor and students. The last point may be the most important. Samuel Johnson, I think, was right about literature: it must instruct while pleasing. We teach literature because we believe the experience of reading it and talking about it stimulates the mind and the soul; unless reading literature is enjoyable, however, most people will not bother to experience it.

Works Cited

Bartholomae, David, and Anthony R. Petrosky, eds. *Facts, Artifacts, and Counterfacts: Theory and Method for a Reading and Writing Course*. Upper Montclair, NJ: Boynton/Cook, 1986.

Bean, John C. *Engaging Ideas: The Professor's Guide to Integrating Writing, Critical Thinking, and Active Learning in the Classroom*. San Francisco: Jossey-Bass, 1996.

Bogdan, Deanne. (1988). Abstract of position paper "Romancing the Response: Issues of Engagement and Detachment in Reading Literature." ERIC Item: ED298498. Accessed 10 July 1998 <http://ericir.syr.edu/>.

Bonwell, Charles C., and James A. Eison. *Active Learning: Creating Excitement in the Classroom*. ASHE-ERIC Higher Education Report. Washington: George Washington University School of Education and Human Development, 1991.

Bradbury, Ray. *Fahrenheit 451*. New York: Ballantine, 1991.

Burke, Kenneth. *A Grammar of Motives*. New York: Prentice-Hall, 1945.

———. *A Rhetoric of Motives*. New York: Prentice-Hall, 1950.

Frye, Northrop. *Anatomy of Criticism: Four Essays*. Princeton: Princeton UP, 1957.

Kinneavy, James L. *A Theory of Discourse: The Aims of Discourse*. Englewood Cliffs, NJ: Prentice-Hall, 1971.

Kirsch, Gesa, and Patricia A. Sullivan. *Methods and Methodologies in Composition Research*. Carbondale: Southern Illinois UP, 1992.

Lauer, Janice M., and J. William Asher. *Composition Research: Empirical Designs*. New York: Oxford UP, 1988.

Lovitt, Carl R. "Using Journals to Redefine Public and Private Domains in the Literature Classroom." *When Writing Teachers Teach Literature*. Ed. Art Young and Toby Fulwiler. Portsmouth, NH: Heinemann-Boynton/Cook, 1995. 230–44.

Pianko, S. H. "A Description of the Composing Processes of College Freshman Writers." *Research in the Teaching of English* 13.1 (1979): 5–22.

Scholes, Robert. *Textual Power: Literary Theory and the Teaching of English*. New Haven, CT: Yale UP, 1985.

Stice, James E. "A Teaching Effectiveness Workshop." [Workshop materials.] Rapid City, SD: August 1995.

Tedards, Douglas, M. "Journal Writing and the Study of Poetry." *When Writing Teachers Teach Literature*. Ed. Art Young and Toby Fulwiler. Portsmouth, NH: Heinemann-Boynton/Cook, 1995. 217–28.

Whitehead, Alfred North. *The Aims of Education and Other Essays*. New York: Free, 1967.

Appendix: Playing Twenty Questions with Literature— Heuristics for the Exploration of Literary Texts

Criticism is a lens which allows us to focus on certain aspects of the text. At the same time, all critical approaches, while promoting insight, impose partial blindness. This is because each system focuses our attention on certain aspects of and relationships to the text, while drawing attention away from others, effectively (if temporarily) silencing them. Another way of looking at critical systems is that each approach is a heuristic, allowing us to brainstorm about the text by providing us with a set of guidelines for exploring a text, often a set of questions and a guiding philosophy (or agenda, if you want to be political about it). I do not believe it is possible to create a complete system of literary analysis to cover every possible way of looking at every possible text. Every system—and, of course, every critique—will be incomplete; but without these approaches, our ability to explore, understand, enjoy, and value literary texts (whatever "literary" really means) would be greatly reduced. Here, then, are twenty questions one can ask about novels, films, plays, and perhaps even poems. I offer them as a starting point for exploration. Enjoy.

1. Questions of Plot and Structure

I have sometimes argued that the six basic plots are as follows:

- Boy Meets Girl, or Girl Meets Boy, or Boy Meets Boy, or Girl Meets Girl . . .
- Boy or Girl Saves World (or at least his or her little corner of it)
- Boy or Girl Learns Better (or Boy or Girl Grows Up)
- Boy or Girl Goes on Quest
- Boy or Girl Goes Home (or finds a home that he or she might not even have been looking for)

- Boy or Girl Gets Killed (and probably never had a chance to do anything about it)

There is also the dramatic framework set up by Northrop Frye and others:

- **Spring/Comedy/Conservative.** Hero succeeds in reforming a corrupt society of some kind in romance and/or other personal endeavors. The story line is considered conservative because it suggests that our society is basically all right at the core, although individual injustices must be met and defeated (and that this can be done through wit and the uncovering of hypocrisy and vanity rather than through action, particularly radical, large-scale, systematic, or violent action).

- **Summer/Romance/Anarchistic.** Hero abandons or fails to reform a corrupt society but succeeds in romance. The genre is considered anarchistic because it presumes that victory can take place only on the level of personal success or failure; often, the best way to deal with a corrupt society is to simply go away, to escape and create one's own society. In Frye's view, people win even if the world around them falls apart. In other words, people don't need society in order to be good or happy.

- **Autumn/Tragedy/Radical.** Hero restores order but is destroyed or endures personal loss because of it; the genre is considered radical because it suggests that changes in society can be made, should be made, must be made with action, and must be made even at great personal cost.

- **Winter/Satire/Liberal.** Hero neither restores order nor succeeds in personal goals; often the hero is as corrupt as the society he or she would, in other genres, be attempting to reform; or he or she becomes corrupt in the attempt to create reform. The genre is considered "liberal" because it suggests that political change is a myth, that no change in the system will produce fundamental changes in society—although perhaps we can achieve small victories by living well—but we must accept an "I'm okay, you're okay" attitude about things and accept that heroic plans to make big changes are doomed to failure.

It is important, by the way, to keep the political aspect of literature in mind. *Nothing is more political than literature,* even when it overtly makes an argument about a particular political issue, because so much of literature is concerned with power and morality, about what is true, good, and possible, about what is just and beautiful, about who has power and who should have power in society and in the family, and about how that power should be employed, and for what ends. It is hard to find a work of literature that does not ask us to join with or join against certain characters (or the narrator); in doing this, a work of literature becomes an argument for (or against) a particular political, ethical, social, and/or moral agenda.

In "The Last Waltz," Stephen King (yes, that Stephen King) talks about novels as being about the conflict between order and disorder. He describes his horror novels as Apollonian (orderly, sober, normal, sane) societies being attacked or destroyed by some Dionysian (disorderly, drunken, abnormal, insane) element.

Another idea is that of the text as verbal object, as self-contained universe of verbal logic, whose artistic impact comes not so much from the ideas themselves but from how those ideas and characters operate as a self-contained system, in the way that a symphony is not so much about tone but about structures of tones, and the way a sculpture is not so much about image as about the cooperation of many images to create a single effect ("objective criticism").

Finally, it is worth considering a work from the perspective of Kinneavian theory. James L. Kinneavy argues in *A Theory of Discourse* that there are really four basic kinds of human communication. Expressive discourse emphasizes the views and feelings of the writer. Referential discourse emphasizes the topic being discussed. Persuasive discourse emphasizes the audience, as it is composed with the intention of discussing the topic to influence the audience in some manner. And literary discourse emphasizes the language itself, with the goal of creating an artistic construct that will entertain the audience. (It is interesting that Cicero defines rhetoric as having three goals: to instruct, to move, and to please, which sound similar to the effects of referential, persuasive, and literary discourse.) Every text, Kinneavy says, may contain elements of any of these four goals; so any work of literature can be examined in terms of expression, reference, persuasion, and literary creation.

2. Questions of Motifs and Symbols

Motifs are another important aspect of fictional form. Images or themes may be repeated or, as often occurs in music, employed as a series of variations on a central image or theme. As in cluster criticism (discussed in section 6 below), the use may not have to refer to any meaning outside the text, although in some cases this is of central importance to the meaning and impact of the text; but it is always true that motifs create a sense of connection between different aspects or moments in the text itself. For example, if we know that roses are important to the hero, any use of roses or rose imagery may be a sign of this kind of connection.

Symbols are, of course, a central aspect of literature. Anything that is not literally what it is, that may have some hidden meaning or meanings, can be a symbol. Symbols, of course, can be used to create a resonance or connection of meaning(s) throughout the text through repetition and variation.

3. Questions of Character

A system outlined by Northrop Frye (see *Anatomy of Criticism*, pages 172–73) posits four basic character types. The first is the *eiron* (the self-deprecator). There are several kinds of eirons, including the neutral hero or heroine and the witty sidekick (originally in Roman drama, this was a tricky slave—if you've seen Marty Feldman in the film *Young Frankenstein*, you get the idea). Other types of characters in Frye's discussion of drama (which to some degree can probably cross over to fiction) are the following: the *alazon* (the blocking force, often a hypocritical boaster, and sometimes a father figure in competition with the hero for the girl—Frye points out that comedies often combine both sexual and political triumphs, e.g., perhaps most commonly boy saves world and gets girl); the *buffoon* (who increases the festivity of the mood rather than contributing to the story); and the *churl* (sometimes a "straight man," often a naive rustic, sometimes simply someone who refuses to enter into the cheerful spirit of events).

4. Questions of Style

Style is one of those fuzzy terms that can mean many things. It is, however, worth considering the actual diction, syntax, and presentation of the text. This can cover an enormous range of textual features, including the length and complexity of sentences, the variation of sentence forms, the relative degree of abstract or concrete language employed by the text, the use of images, the length of paragraphs, pacing, the division of the text in chapters or sections, even the physical layout and production values of the text (e.g., the size and font of the typeface, the quality of paper used), although this last may be outside the control of the author. All of these factors can influence how we experience the text, how realistic we find the story, how we view the characters and their actions, and so on.

5. Questions of Genre (Definition)

Genre literally means "kind" or "class." Almost every text can be described as belonging to one or more genres; the few texts—if any exist

—that are unclassifiable can still be approached based on the genres to which they may be responses (including rejections). Genres are useful to readers and critics because every genre establishes a set of guidelines and expectations about the text's form, content, and goal, and about people who are allowed to create such texts in the first place, people who are supposed to read the text once it is completed, how important the text is, what themes might be explored in the text, and so on. Some basic questions include the following: What makes this a "novel," as opposed to some other form, such as a novelette, an epic, a drama, a ballad poem (in prose form), and so on? What makes this a certain kind of novel, e.g., historical, Western, science fiction, fantasy, romance, or mystery? Is the essential dramatic quality of the story comedic, tragic, romantic, or satiric?

6. Burkean Approaches to Literature

This is the notion of form as the arousal and fulfillment of expectations (from Kenneth Burke). What expectations does the text create and how does it ultimately fulfill them, if indeed it does so?

We can also employ a tool referred to by Burke as the pentad. It addresses any dramatic (or fictional) work by looking at any action within the text as a combination of agent, agency, act, purpose, and scene. Who did it? By what means? What did he or she do? Why? Where and when? (See Burke's *A Grammar of Motives* and *A Rhetoric of Motives* for more information.) One important aspect of the pentad is that by breaking the fiction down into its dramatistic elements, we can see which ones are most important to an author (for example, if circumstances drive a character to certain actions, if "scene" rather than "agent" or "purpose" determines the "act," then this tells us something about the way the author views and is portraying reality). In addition, Burke talks about "identification," by which he means how one thing is associated (or identified) with other things. This concept is useful in determining how the author creates certain effects or feelings in the audience. For example, repeated images of life are used to describe books in *Fahrenheit 451*. Identifying books and their ideas with life and living things illustrates symbolism that works on several levels: books and ideas are the "life" of a society, ideas are "alive," and books are not simply dead pieces of paper and cardboard but living things because of the ideas contained within them.

Related to all this is another form of criticism designed by Burke called cluster criticism. Here one looks for clusters of terms, themes, and images and attempts to outline the network of connections between them. This type of examination focuses not on how the clustered items refer to established meanings of ideas outside the text; what matters is that within the text they are creating their own interlocked system of meanings.

7. Questions of Heroism, Villainy, and Monstrosity, of Good and Evil (Quality)

I tend to agree with John Gardner that literature is not only political, but moral. Every work of literature can be examined in terms of its statements about good and evil. Every work of literature can be treated as an argument, explicit or implicit, in favor of certain kinds of thinking and certain kinds of behavior, and as an argument against other kinds of thinking and behavior. In addition, one can examine the text as making an argument about what is normal/natural and what is abnormal/ unnatural. Some questions that get at such concerns are as follows: Who are the heroic figures and why? What is the author trying to say about the nature of humanity and heroism that leads him or her to make these people the heroic figures? How heroic is the protagonist? The antagonist? What is the author trying to say by using heroic and unheroic figures in these positions within the story? Who are the villainous figures and what makes them villainous? Who are the antiheroic figures? What makes them antiheroic? Is it simply a quality of being somehow ordinary, normal, or the like? Who are the monstrous figures? What makes them monstrous (as opposed to "evil")?

8. Questions of Authorial Expression, Ideology, and Psychology (Expressive Criticism)

What can we learn about the author's views by examining the text? What is the author trying to say about concerns such as the nature of heroism, beauty, truth, reality, or justice in this text? How is the text typical or atypical of a particular author's works or expressed viewpoints? How does it show his or her growth or progress as an author?

9. Questions of Reality and Depiction (Mimetic Criticism)

One approach to literature is to examine the relationship between "art" and the "real world," between "art" and "truth." A great deal has been written about whether art should be "truthful" or not, whether realism is the real measure of art, or whether art is more "real" than reality because it allows us to see the essence of things that we can experience only in terms of material or social aspects. Some questions that might be considered are these: What view of the world is being presented in the text? How "realistic" is the text and why do we believe it to be realistic? How does the style and arrangement of the text serve to create or destroy a sense of realism (or surrealism)?

10. Questions of Narration and Silence (Viewpoint)

Every story is narrated. Someone, whether it is one of the characters in the story, or an unseen narrator, or the point of view provided by a film's director, is relating the events of the tale to us, letting us experience those events in one particular way while blocking out other viewpoints. This blocking out of alternatives is usually not malicious, although authors are frequently aware of the significance of having the story told from one point of view and not another. Ultimately, the choice of one narrator over another is unavoidable; there is no way for a single narrator or author to present the totality of everything that takes place in a story, but we need to be aware that every story could be told in an infinite number of ways. Some of the questions one can consider include the following: Who is telling the story and how does that influence how the story gets told? What narrative techniques are being used and how does that influence the way the story is told? Who is not getting to speak and how do they influence how we view the story and the ideas it contains? Whose point of view is being valorized? Whose point of view is being silenced?

11. Questions of Change (Process, History, and Relationship with Text)

Novels and dramas are dynamic forms of literature; almost always, the action described by a novel or a play takes place over a period of time and describes some kind of change. So we can look at the following: How does the plot develop? We are used to the traditional description of plot as one of introduction, crisis, climax, and anticlimax or conclusion (although in some non-Western societies we do not see this kind of plot development, an absence that suggests a more spatial/static relationship with the world rather than the dynamic/process/progress/change-oriented relationship common in Western societies). How do things change in the novel? In particular, how do people change? Orson Scott Card has said (in a public talk at a science fiction convention, the specific occasion of which now escapes me) that his main character is always "the person in the most pain," implying that the story is not over until that pain is somehow resolved. (Gardner talks about writing as a response to woundedness.) Who or what is responsible for the changes that take place?

Another issue is that we are involved in a relationship with the text. Consider the very process of your reading of the text. How have you changed (in knowledge, in attitude, or in other ways), *if* you have changed, during the course of reading the text, and now, afterwards, having finished it?

12. Questions of Rhetoric (Rhetorical Criticism)

Every text can be treated as an argument, explicit or implicit, for certain things. The author wants us to believe certain things or do certain things. The author wants us to feel certain things about certain characters. The author wants us to experience the ideas and themes of the story in a certain way. How does all this happen? How does the text operate as an explicit or implicit argument for a certain agenda? What is the author trying to prove and how does he or she go about proving it? How successful is the text as an explicit or implicit argument? Why does it succeed (or fail)?

A related issue is that of the text as a semiotic or sign system: How does it go about communicating its meaning to the audience, and, specifically, how does it operate as or within a system of symbols?

Adapting the classical approach to literature treats the text as speech:

- **Ethos:** Who is the "narrator," and (why) do we trust both the narrator and mode of presentation? What relationship is established between text/narrator and audience?

- **Logos:** What ideas are established and how are they established, implied, or proved?

- **Pathos:** How does the author (through the narrator and/or the events of the text) appeal to the audience's values or emotions? Why is this done? What does the author hope to accomplish by doing this? How does it help in his or her attempt to persuade the audience?

Kenneth Burke's pentad and notion of identification are also valuable for considering how a text might attempt to persuade or argue with an audience. What kind of dramatic structures are being set up in the text, what is being identified with what, and for what purpose?

Finally, one can consider how a text might influence an audience in ways the author might not have originally intended. For example: Do slasher films encourage violence towards women? If so, how?

13. Questions of Race, Gender, and Class (Multicultural, Feminist, and Marxist Criticism)

This is a cluster of questions related to the views of the author and the possible influence of the text on topics concerning power and relationships between different groups of people in society. What does the text say about masculine and feminine roles in society? What does the text say about the relationship between races and the concept of race? What does the text say about working-class people, "white collar" workers, bosses and laborers, masters and slaves, relationships between classes, and the very concept of class?

14. Questions of Canon ("But is it art?")

Every text can be examined in relationship with a canon, a hierarchy of works considered the core of a genre, either because of quality, originality, influence, or representativeness. Those most central to the canon are those considered to represent what that culture or discourse community considers best and most beautiful among a certain set of texts; they reflect ideological assumptions about a genre or a set of genres. What place does any specific text have within that hierarchy? Is it primary, secondary, minor, marginal, or outside the canon? What place should it have? If it does not hold such a place, why do you think this is so?

15. Questions of Culture (Cultural Criticism)

What does the text tell us, either directly or by implication, about the society in which it was composed or the audiences for whom it was intended?

Ideology here refers to the underlying assumptions that individuals and groups make about what is true, good, and possible (and the opposite: what is false, bad, and impossible). All people and all groups have some kind of ideology, although certain ideologies are more flexible than others. In addition, ideologies are often "invisible," that is, the assumptions are so basic to our understanding of reality that we are not aware of them or, if we are aware of them, we never think of questioning them.

Regardless of what the text seems to say on the surface, what appear to be the ideological assumptions that the text is based upon? What can we say about the community in which the text was originally written? What can we say about the community for which the text was written? (Authors who write for "the universal audience" still have some assumptions about what that audience is and what they expect, and will write in reaction to these assumptions.) The image we might use here is the text as a window onto the lives and minds of a particular culture.

The terms *community* and *culture* can refer to any group of people who share a set of assumptions about the true, the good, and the possible. Many critics and philosophers use the term "discourse community." This is because (1) they believe that all communities are discourse communities, since people can operate as groups only through the use of language and texts in the first place—as I recall, Cicero made this argument about two thousand years ago—and (2) because the word *community* by itself may imply the idea of "people who share only a physical and temporal locale." But the ideas and emotions shared through written texts can and do cross physical and temporal boundaries—we can "know" someone (or have an argument with him or her) through what he or she has written even if we never meet the individual personally.

16. Questions of Morality—or Ethics ("Is it good art?")

Many critics believe that literature must have a moral or ethical component. Samuel Johnson complained about the new genre of the novel in the eighteenth century because he was concerned about it being a bad moral influence. He and other writers believed that true art instructs while pleasing. John Gardner believed that literature, real art, must be "life-affirming." To what extent does the text teach, and what does it teach, and do you believe it is a good thing that the text is teaching these ideas? Why or why not? (Often, questions about what is erotic or pornographic are based on the notion that real art must be life-affirming.)

17. Questions of Intertextuality and Deconstruction (Metatextuality)

Many critics are interested in the metatextual aspects of a piece of art. Modern linguistic theory argues that linguistic meaning takes place within the "free play between signifiers," that is, words are meaningful not only because they refer to something in the world, but because of their place in the enormous network of meaning that is a language. In fact, words have meaning because of their difference from other meanings. For example, the word "cat" can refer to an actual cat in part because it does not refer to what the word "dog" indicates, or the word "squirrel," and so on. But if this is true, if there is no "center of language," no final anchor of meaning, then texts can be approached by asking how the meaning of the text "deconstructs" itself through the internal contradictions created by assuming any final structure of language or meaning.

Another issue to consider is whether (and if so how) the text calls attention to its existence as a text, rather than being a text that pretends to be a literal translation of reality into a linguistic structure.

18. Questions of Traditions, Periods, and Locales

These questions and those in the next category view the text within a larger context of other texts and works of art. One way to do this is to consider the fact that texts are responses not only to the real world but also to other texts, which they may imitate, draw upon, react to, refer to, and so on. In other words, texts have meaning to us because we have read other texts; so the relationship, implied or explicit between a text and other texts, in or out of its own genre, is worth exploring. For example, how does our concept of the monster Grendel influence (and get influenced by) our notion of the Frankenstein monster, both as he appears in the novel and as he is rendered in later film versions?

Another way of looking at this issue is to ask what literary or aesthetic or rhetorical traditions the text belongs to and how it fits into those traditions. What does it mean, for example, to say that a novelist has written an "absurdist play" or a "picaresque novel"? One can argue about whether *tradition* is another name for *genre*, but it is sometimes useful to treat the two issues as separate.

Finally, it is worth asking how a text relates to the culture in which and for which it was produced. How is a text typical (or atypical) not only of a genre, but of a historical period and locale? For example, to say that James Joyce is a "modern Irish writer" tells us something about him, just as to say that Joyce was an "experimental novelist" also tells us something. What exactly does it mean to say that a writer is typical of a certain period, geographical location, or other cultural grouping?

19. Questions of Comparison and Contrast

This is one of the easiest and broadest of all the questions. Quite simply, one should consider how any particular work is similar to or different from other works. Often, it is by comparing one work with another that the unique features of both works will come into sharp focus. Because this is such a broad question, however, it is often useful to compare the work in question with another work that you are familiar with, and to combine it with other questions from this list, but with only one question at a time. For example, one can explore how the Hero in Shakespeare's *Henry V* differs from Dorimant, the protagonist in the Restoration comedy *The Man of Mode.* Or, one can consider the treatment of evil in *Frankenstein* as compared to the treatment of evil in *To Kill a Mockingbird.*

20. Questions of Reaction (Reader Response)

One of the new theories of criticism is based on the very real notion that we do not simply passively absorb experiences; instead, what we experience as reality is mediated. The raw sensory experience goes through several filters (e.g., sensory, linguistic, cultural), and personal factors such as our desires, quirks, interests, and memories, operate upon the information as we construct what we think reality is. Reading is, in this view, not a simple communication of data; we are as responsible for what we see in the text as the writer who originally transmitted the information. We are all translators. In other words, we do not merely receive information but participate in constructing our understanding of what we have read. For this reason, all individual reactions to the text are potentially valuable. What do you personally think about the text? What do you find in it? Why do you feel this way? Your view is as important as that of any other critic; the only difference between you and the so-called professional critics is often nothing more than that they took a lot more English courses than you have and, as a result, have somewhat more experience (i.e., they have more fully developed their own system for looking at texts).

Want to read more about it? Here are some (but not all) of the authors you should look into:

- Aristotle
- Wayne C. Booth
- Kenneth Burke
- Cicero
- Terry Eagleton
- Michel Foucault
- Northrop Frye
- Paul Fussell
- John Gardner
- Samuel Johnson
- James L. Kinneavy

- Richard Lanham
- Hayden White

For a list of their books, all you have to do is find an online library catalog or online bookstore (there are several you can reach through my "Rhetoric Page" Web site at http://www.kettering.edu/~mgellis/GMI_Rhet.htm).

Works Cited

Bradbury, Ray. *Fahrenheit 451*. New York: Ballantine, 1991.

Cicero. *De Oratore*. Trans. E. W. Sutton and H. Rackham. Loeb Classical Library No. 348–49. Cambridge, MA: Harvard UP, 1942–48.

Frye, Northrop. *Anatomy of Criticism: Four Essays*. Princeton: Princeton UP, 1957.

Gardner, John. *On Moral Fiction*. New York: Basic, 1978.

Johnson, Samuel. "The Rambler." Number 4. *The Yale Edition of the Works of Samuel Johnson*. Vol. 3. Ed. W. J. Bate and Albrecht B. Strauss. New Haven, CT: Yale UP, 1958. 19–25.

King, Stephen. "The Last Waltz—Horror and Morality, Horror in Magic." *Stephen King's Danse Macabre*. New York: Berkley, 1983. 387–409.

Kinneavy, James L. *A Theory of Discourse: The Aims of Discourse*. Englewood Cliffs, NJ: Prentice-Hall, 1971.

3 "But How Do You *Do* That?": Decision Making for the Seminar Facilitator

Michael S. Hale
Appalachian State University

Elizabeth A. City
Harvard University

Leading a discussion in a seminar format seems natural for some people and not so natural for others. Because the role of the teacher is more than simply following a protocol or asking a series of questions, leading a seminar can seem like part science, part art, and part magic. The complexity of the problem leaves some teachers asking, "How do you *do* that?" While we can give no magic formula for leading seminars, we can isolate the decisions that must be made during the seminar in order to answer the question. Able seminar leaders must understand the components of a good seminar, and they must make sound decisions to keep the components in balance.

Just as fishing is more than baiting the hook and casting, there is more to seminar facilitation than basic skills. To help teachers better understand the decision-making process for facilitating seminars, we have identified four key elements to consider. We refer to these elements as fulcrums because they are the leverage points upon which seminars should be balanced. They involve a variety of decisions that teachers need to make in facilitating a successful seminar, including whether to ask another question, what question to ask, and when to remind students of productive behaviors or to refer to the text, along with many other actions or nonactions that might be chosen. The rest of this chapter will describe these fulcrums and discuss how each is essential to seminar instruction.

The Fulcrums

The primary fulcrums we have identified are safety, authentic participation, challenge, and ownership. Each is a necessary condition for the next, so we will discuss the fulcrums in the order in which they should be considered. To use the fulcrums as a guide for increasing the success of seminars in the classroom, a teacher should focus on the first fulcrum, safety, until he or she and the students feel they have created a safe environment. Only after this is accomplished should the primary focus shift to the next fulcrum, authentic participation, and so on.

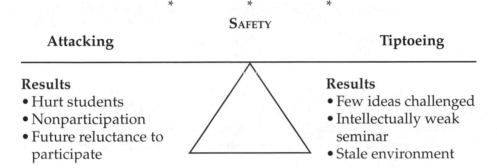

The last seminar in my [Elizabeth City's] seventh-grade humanities class had been a bit dull. The students were just not interested in the text. They had dutifully offered a few ideas, but it had mostly turned into a conversation—or rather, argument—between two students. But today was different. Today everyone was on the edge of their seats, leaning forward, watching each speaker with all the attention of viewing a boxing match. They were looking closely at the text, following each speaker's point, seeing where they could add to someone's point or disagree based on the text. And the conversation! "I can't believe these are seventh graders," I thought to myself. A bit smugly, I congratulated myself that I had made it possible for these students to comment so brilliantly on the role of history in their lives and to ponder the question of why we should study history at all. And I even had a witness. Our dean of instruction had chosen this day to sit in and observe the seminar. As I mentally patted myself on the back, I returned my focus to the conversation. "History is more than what is just written in books," said Kendra (all names are pseudonyms). "It's all around us. Everything we do and has been done before is history." "Okay," said Timothy. "But I don't think history can tell me anything about who I am and who I should become. At the most I should study the history of my own ancestors. I don't need to study people in China or Africa to tell me about my own life." Timothy's comment was met with many head shakes and scattered applause from a few of his classmates. "Timothy, I disagree with you," said Jenna, rather emphatically. She held up a photo of Chinese youth. "This does have something to do with you." As she continued to make her point, several students looked like they might explode with their ideas before they could

share them. Sandy's comment—"Yeah, it's like that thing Mr. Wheeler told us about, a butterfly flapping its wings causing a hurricane on the other side of the world. History is like that. Every little thing affects us in some way, even if we don't know how"—was completely lost in the storm of shouts and applause that erupted as Timothy and Jenna and their supporting casts continued to make their points. The conversation was flying back and forth, around the circle. Students were talking passionately about their ideas. But Sandy had his head in his hands, frustrated that no one had heard his point. Jenna was either going to cry or yell louder. Timothy had resorted to "That's just stupid" to back up his ideas. Antonio slumped in his chair and shot the ceiling a bored "I-get-enough-of-this-yelling-in-my-neighborhood" look. Sharon looked like she had a carefully thought out point to contribute if she could just jump in. Class ended, and the students left the room still talking about the role of history. When I checked in with our dean later, I said, "What did you think?" expecting to hear something about how interesting the conversation was and how impressed he was with the depth of their thinking. Instead he said, "It was a little too Jerry Springer, wasn't it?"

The emotional and psychological safety of students is the first condition necessary for successful seminars. Without an emotionally safe environment, many students simply will not share their ideas about the text. Most students, particularly at the secondary level, are not comfortable enough intellectually to offer ideas about which they are unsure. Given that engaging in a discussion of ideas requires some intellectual risk, it is vital that students feel that they will be protected. Furthermore, the relative safety of a seminar setting can affect the success of future seminars. Only the most talkative, confident, or combative students will participate. To keep this fulcrum balanced, a facilitator must keep the following questions in mind:

- What is the tone of the conversation?
- Are the students showing respect for each other?

The tone of the conversation affects the content of the conversation. When these conversations are cooperative, ideas move forward. When they are contentious, participants may simply dig into their foxholes a little deeper rather than genuinely considering the merit of opposing viewpoints. The students do not need to agree with one another, but they have to respect differences of ideas. In fact, a successful seminar is built on the understanding that emerges from different ideas. Without this respect, a conversation can evolve into a talk-show free-for-all, marked by righteous indignation.

To create and maintain an atmosphere of emotional safety and respect, facilitators must be aware of how both they and the students act and react during the seminar. Prior to the seminar, the tone for a safe environment should have been set during a discussion of the guidelines for seminar participation. The guidelines for seminar are simple—a participant (1) must be prepared for the text, (2) can make statements or ask questions, (3) must listen carefully, (4) must be polite, and (5) should refer to the text for support whenever possible. Of these guidelines, the second and fourth are most critical to creating a safe seminar environment in the sense that a good seminar is a polite but intellectually challenging conversation.

The teacher should also remind the students of her or his role as facilitator of the conversation. This role requires that the teacher neither offer his or her own ideas about the text nor give positive or negative feedback to a particular student. Because students are used to teacher feedback, the lack of it may create an uncomfortable, and consequently unsafe, environment unless students understand the reasons behind its absence. Instead, facilitator feedback during the seminar should concern the degree to which students are following the guidelines of seminar behavior. When providing this type of feedback, seminar leaders need to make it clear to the students that they are stepping out of their role as facilitator and back into the role of teacher.

Many teachers, including the authors, use the term "time-out" to signify to students this change of roles. During the time-out, the teacher might ask students what they were doing well during the seminar and what they needed to work on, or might point out instances of students politely disagreeing with others. This reminder might be reinforced by a role-playing exercise in which students model the way a respectful conversation takes place. The teacher can then call "time-in" to return to the seminar and her or his role as facilitator.

Seminar is a time when sarcasm is rarely, if ever, permitted. Humor is certainly acceptable, but not at the expense of others. This restriction can be difficult for high school students, who often defend their own insecurities by attacking the vulnerability of others. Attacking people is never appropriate in seminar; challenging other people's ideas, however, is vital for increasing understanding (Strong 56). An atmosphere must develop in which all ideas can be discussed and challenged without students feeling personally attacked.

Before moving on to the other fulcrums, the facilitator must create a climate that allows students to share ideas, hear each other speak, and challenge each other's ideas. Some students may take longer than others to learn to respect other students and the seminar process; however, it is essential that safety be established before the facilitator begins to focus on authentic participation.

*   *   *

AUTHENTIC PARTICIPATION

Nonparticipation or Egocentric Participation		Inauthentic Participation

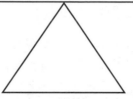

Results		**Results**
• Silent students		•Mere talking
• Unfocused students		•Idea hopping
• Little interaction among participants		•Expert-parroting

I sat in a large gym with a group of teachers who had gathered for a day of professional development and reflection. Only a couple of the teachers had participated in a seminar before, so we chose a text that would be accessible—Neil Postman's "My Graduation Speech" (readily available on the Web). Before we began the seminar, the teachers diligently marked up their texts, underlining, commenting, and questioning as they read. I asked them to share ideas with a partner before we began, and there was a loud buzz of ideas. We then went around the seminar circle, with each person sharing two words that captured the people featured in the speech. I followed with my standard first line: "Now I'm just going to open it up for anyone who would like to explain why they chose the words they did or has something else to say about the text." And then I waited. And waited. And waited. "Shoot," I thought. "I forgot to warn them that I will outwait them during silence, so they needn't wait for me to rescue them." I even started getting a little nervous as the clock ticked on. As I waited, I thought back to when I had done a seminar on this same text with my ninth-grade students not too long ago. With them the problem was not so much silence as it was not enough silence. They jumped right in with the first line, but bounced around the text like Tigger. Each student had his or her own idea and waited patiently to share it. Robert, for example, caught himself several times as he started to interrupt people. Eventually, he found an opening and shared his idea with pride. Unfortunately, the conversation had already taken four turns away from his idea, but he had been so anxious to share his thought that he didn't listen to other people's thoughts. The conversation hopped from one line of text to the other, with few linkages. The students were almost there but didn't want to dive deeply into any particular issue. Back with my adults,

I reassured myself that they had each had much to say to their partner not two minutes ago. Sure enough, someone finally breathed deeply and said, "Well I chose 'enduring' because . . ."

This fulcrum balances mere talking and silence. The middle ground is authentic participation, defined by deliberate, thoughtful, and selective contributions from the participants. In the seminars recounted above, the adults, though silent for a period, were authentically participating; the students, on the other hand, were not, despite much sharing of comments. The student seminar is typical of a class that has recently established a climate of safety. A class at this stage of development has often not yet learned to focus their conversation but is ready to learn to participate authentically.

Once they realize that it is safe to do so, some students will make statements simply to seek attention or because they know they are supposed to, not because they have genuinely reflected upon the ideas in the text. However, once focused on this fulcrum, the seminar facilitator can easily gauge the authenticity of the seminar and help students concentrate on the task of developing a deeper understanding of the text. Some of the questions a facilitator must keep in mind to balance this fulcrum are the following:

- Are many students participating primarily to seek attention?
- Is the conversation text-focused?
- Are the students jumping from comment to comment without exploring them in depth?
- Is the talking merely a sharing of ideas, or are students responding to one another?

Most teachers can recognize when a student is participating simply to gain attention. The facilitator's response to this type of participation should often be to ask the student, "Can you show us where you find support for that in the text?" Asking students to support their answers will force most students to engage with the text and find some linkage to their comment or simply to pull out of the conversation until they find some connection to the text.

When inauthentic individual comments are made during a focused conversation, the facilitator should address them directly only if students are becoming distracted and the conversation is in danger of being derailed. If students ignore the inauthentic comments, then the facilitator should simply write them down in his or her notes and discuss authentic participation with the individual student at a later time.

Another common developmental stage of seminar occurs when many students jump from idea to idea with few connections among statements. The result is a seminar with an extremely active discussion that doesn't result in a greater understanding of the text. The energy level can be very high in such discussions, but it is important to keep in mind that a deep conversation of ideas generates its own energy. A good seminar is marked by reflective activity.

Reflective activity is rarely honored in a group setting or as an aspect of discussions. By reflective activity we mean thoughtfulness (in the sense of one's being full of thought) put into action through the spoken word. In a seminar this means that, before speaking, students should consider both the text and what others have said.

A good seminar may be marked by periods of silence that last for up to one or two minutes. A period of silence this long is fine as long as students use it to think about the text. When silence fills the air during a discussion in a typical classroom, it is often broken by a teacher asking another question or adding expert knowledge about the topic. Although this type of classroom interaction may be appropriate for some discussions, it frees students from the necessary burden of generating their own thoughts and ideas about the text at hand. Students may shift into cognitive neutral if they know the teacher will fill the silence; however, if the teacher as facilitator is patient and waits for students to break the silence, the rewards are often a conversation of much greater depth.

All pauses in the conversation, however, are not the result of reflection time. Sometimes students need a probing question or need to move to a different idea in the text. Thus, the facilitator must consider why there is silence. Is it because the current line of thinking has been completely explored, or is it because the students are waiting to be given the correct answer? If the former, then the facilitator might need to ask a question that encourages students to consider a different idea in the text or to consider their current line of thinking in light of some other part of the text. If, however, the students simply need to go back and review more of the text, then promoting reflection through silence is an effective facilitator response.

The final indicator of authentic participation is whether the students are talking directly to the facilitator or to each other. Until they cease to look to the facilitator after every comment, the conversation will never develop into a natural conversation. The group may occasionally need a reminder that the seminar is their conversation, not the facilitator's. Once students understand how to participate authentically, it is time to begin focusing on the challenge of the seminar.

* * *

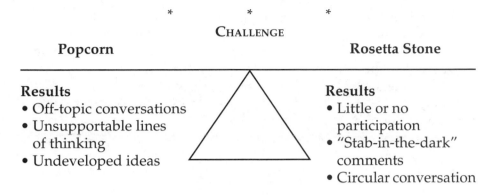

CHALLENGE

Popcorn   **Rosetta Stone**

Results
- Off-topic conversations
- Unsupportable lines of thinking
- Undeveloped ideas

Results
- Little or no participation
- "Stab-in-the-dark" comments
- Circular conversation

My seventh graders were at it again, this time in a much more respectful manner while delving into Horace Miner's "Body Ritual among the Nacirema." They were deep into a discussion about what it means to be "civilized" and had been carefully distinguishing between "uncivilized" and "primitive" for many minutes. Again, I mapped the conversation furiously, fascinated by their conversation. I jumped in to summarize the definitions and differences they had established between "uncivilized" and "primitive." The conversation moved on to another point as they built on their definitions. About fifteen minutes later, Christine, one of my most hard-working and highly achieving students, looked at me and said, "Could you say what the difference between 'uncivilized' and 'primitive' is again? I don't get it." I was almost annoyed. She was way behind in the conversation. We had gone over it thoroughly. Wasn't she paying attention? Then I looked around the circle quickly. "Ellen, no side conversations." I shot Ellen a look that said "you shouldn't do that in seminar," to which she protested, "But I'm confused!" Well, you should have been listening, I thought. Mark had been drawing for several minutes, and Keenan would only contribute, "Well, I think, I think—I don't know what I think," as if to hear his voice for as long as possible. I looked back at Christine's face and saw that she earnestly wanted to understand. I took a deep breath, made eye contact with Christine, Ellen, Mark, and Keenan, and said, "Well, as we said, 'uncivilized' means . . ."

Because most classrooms include students with a wide range of experiences and intellectual development, this can be a difficult fulcrum for the facilitator. Both the questions and the text must be challenging enough to force even the most intellectually mature student to stretch his or her mind, without being beyond comprehension by the least mature student. To maintain this balance, the facilitator must monitor the relative understanding of all students.

To monitor this understanding, the facilitator must be closely attuned to more than just the students who are talking; she or he must also focus on who is daydreaming, aching to speak, talking to a neighbor, or looking bewildered. There are a number of ways to do this, such as taking notes or periodically scanning the room to observe participants (or nonparticipants). Questions to consider when monitoring for this fulcrum include the following:

- Are the same points being made over and over in different words?
- Are only a few students participating?
- Do questions require the students to stop and reflect and return to the text?

At the center of all conversation in a seminar should be the ideas evoked by the text. Assuming the chosen text is rich in ideas, the facilitator must work to help participants focus the conversation on ideas in the text. The goal is to avoid having students talk about topics unrelated to the text, or, at the other end of the spectrum, spend too much time discussing only one idea.

In the case of the slow-moving seminar discussion during which few students are making statements or asking questions, the facilitator has to determine whether the question asked was at too high a level for that particular time during the seminar. To determine whether the students are conceptually unprepared for the question, the facilitator needs to scan the room for looks of befuddlement or complete lack of engagement. If the facilitator decides that confusion is the rule, then he or she should try to ask the question in a different way or break the question down into component parts. To break the question down, the facilitator might ask whether there are certain concepts that the students need help in understanding. For example, in a seminar on Gwendolyn Brooks's "To the Diaspora," when one student asked, "Why do you think Brooks spelled Afrika with a 'k'?," the class responded with silence. The facilitator thought it was a marvelous question but realized by the many blank looks she saw that the other students were not yet ready to attempt plausible answers. She guided the conversation to a different question by saying, "What an interesting question, Chris. I'm not sure we're ready to think about that yet. Let's think about who the speaker of the poem and the audience for the poem might be and then we can return to the question of why Afrika is spelled with a 'k.'"

Off-topic conversations are a common occurrence during seminars, and a facilitator needs to handle them in a way that will lead the conversation back to the ideas in the text. First, a facilitator needs to recognize an off-topic conversation. In most cases this is obvious. For example, during a tenth-grade seminar on Langston Hughes's poem "Theme for English B," a student may begin talking about how his Aunt Edith went to New York once and how much he used to love to play with Aunt Edith's dog when she came to visit. In a case such as this, a facilitator needs to redirect the conversation. For example, she might say: "That's very interesting, William; however, Julie [another student] thought Hughes believed that New York was an important part of who he was—what do any of you think about her assertion?" If the group seems to need frequent reminders about the focus of a seminar, the facilitator might say: "Please remember that a seminar is a conversation focused on the ideas in a text. Now, what do you think the teacher's assessment of Hughes's theme paper was?"

There are also times in a seminar when students are focused on one idea. In such a case the facilitator should address this question: Are students continuing to develop a deeper and more complex understanding of the idea, or are they continually restating the same assertions using different words? If the conversation is continuing to develop a more complex understanding of an idea, then the chances are high that at least some students are being intellectually challenged. To assist the rest, the facilitator might try restating some of the assertions to ensure that all participants are better able to follow the conversation.

If the conversation is not continuing to deepen, the facilitator needs to determine whether to have the students probe the idea more deeply by asking a more challenging question, or by asking students to present evidence for their claims (Adler, *The Paideia Program*; Roberts). Examples of this type of question include "Can you tell me what support you find for that idea?" and "How do you think this fits with the idea of happiness you developed earlier in the conversation?"

Alternately, it may be time to ask a question that moves the conversation to a different idea in the text. For example, during one seminar on the Preamble to the Constitution, students had been discussing the idea of freedom for more than twenty minutes but hadn't moved beyond restating in a variety of ways that "freedom" means one can do whatever one wants to do. To move the conversation along, a facilitator might simply have asked: "How do you think 'freedom' fits with 'justice' in the Preamble?" This would have encouraged participants to consider a new idea in light of their current conversation and provided an opportunity to add depth and nuance to the conversation.

Challenge is balanced when students begin to recognize that all interpretations of the text are not equal; some are more plausible than others, and it is the students' role to discuss the most plausible and reject the least plausible. For example, an assertion that Hughes's "Theme for English B" is a complaint about his instructor's grading practices would be rather difficult to support. On the other hand, an assertion that Hughes was attempting to convey his frustration with his instructor's expectations of him is a considerably more plausible interpretation of the text and would be worthy of discussion. A desired outcome of the seminar process, then, is that experienced participants will recognize more plausible interpretations of texts and eventually abandon less plausible readings.

*   *   *

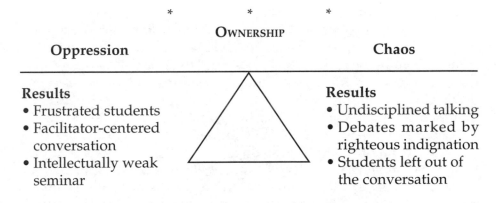

OWNERSHIP

Oppression   **Chaos**

Results
- Frustrated students
- Facilitator-centered conversation
- Intellectually weak seminar

Results
- Undisciplined talking
- Debates marked by righteous indignation
- Students left out of the conversation

Finally, I tore myself away from my own classes and observed another teacher at my school leading a seminar. Her eighth-grade students were very respectful and made several references to the text, Martin Luther King's "I Have a Dream" speech. The students were interested in the text and seemed to have many ideas about it. They were politely saying "I disagree with your point," they probed different ideas in the text, and they obviously wanted to struggle with difficult issues in the text. Clearly, Ms. Green had safety, authentic participation, and challenge at a comfortable balance in her classroom. But something was missing. The students weren't really talking to each other. Ms. Green would ask a question, two students would answer it, and Ms. Green would go back to her prepared list of questions and offer another one. They were open and challenging questions, but the conversation was not open for long before it moved on to something else, and the moving on was always a result of Ms. Green's next question, rather than a student question or comment. At one point, the students started to talk about something in depth, and Ms. Green broke in at a pause to ask her next question. The students looked at her in a funny way since her question had nothing to do with their current conversation, but they dutifully attempted to answer her new question. I felt as if she should be sitting in the center of the circle. I wished I could put Jerome, one of my seventh graders, into her seminar. During our last seminar, Jerome had paused about ten minutes into the conversation and asked a particularly insightful question that hadn't occurred to me. "What a great question," I thought to myself—and I opened with it in my seminar with the next class. Jerome is a questioner and synthesizer, and several of his classmates follow his lead. They've even proposed that I leave the seminar altogether as facilitator. I wondered what Ms. Green would think of that.

This is perhaps the most difficult fulcrum to maintain in balance, particularly for the inexperienced facilitator; however, successful seminar discussions should give students the feeling that they have *ownership* of the ideas explored and generated. The students should be doing the intellectual "heavy lifting" during the seminar. This doesn't just mean that students do all of the talking; rather, it means that they do most of the analysis and evaluation. This expectation presents a challenge for the facilitator. When a discussion moves slowly, the facilitator must consider whether to ask another question or wait for students to find a solid handle on the text that they can use to carry it.

Although this fulcrum is related to *authentic participation* and *challenge*, it is focused more on decreasing the facilitator focus of the seminar while increasing the quality of the discussion. It is listed last because it is the most advanced fulcrum to learn to balance. The questions a facilitator must consider for balancing this fulcrum are these:

- Who is asking the most critical questions?
- Who is determining the direction of the seminar?
- Who is taking the primary responsibility for the integrity of the conversation?

The answer to all of the questions above should be "the students." Until the correct balances have been established between safety, authentic participation, and challenge, the facilitator will have to remain a driving force in the seminar. When the group is ready to begin driving on its own, the facilitator must be ready to give up the wheel.

From the very first seminar, the facilitator must remind students that it is their conversation and their responsibility to find an interpretation of the text. As a group, the goal is a critical evaluation of the ideas in the text. Some facilitators don't trust themselves and/or their students enough to follow the flow of the conversation, especially if it has veered far from what the facilitator had envisioned. As long as the conversation is still focused on the text, however, such an unexpected direction is okay.

It can be difficult for some facilitators to relinquish direct control of the seminar. There are two primary reasons for this difficulty: a facilitator having trouble with any activity in which she or he is not the primary focus, or a facilitator being wedded to a particular line of inquiry for students to explore. An unwillingness to relinquish control of a discussion may be the result of a teacher facilitating a text about which he or she has too deep a personal investment. It is the students' ownership of the text, however, that must receive primary consideration.

It's Ultimately about Trust

In the end, leading seminars requires trust. Facilitators must trust the process they have established, trust the value of the text they have selected, trust their students to recognize significant ideas, trust themselves to make good decisions during the seminar. Attention to the four fulcrums—safety, authentic participation, challenge, and ownership—will help demystify the process of leading seminars and clarify the facilitation of student-centered discussion. Successful facilitators balance seminars on these four fulcrums, perhaps without even realizing that they are doing it. Giving conscious attention to these concerns will not ensure magic, but it will provide answers to the question, "How do you do that?"

Works Cited

Adler, Mortimer J., ed. *The Paideia Program: An Educational Syllabus*. New York: MacMillan, 1984.

———, ed. *The Paideia Proposal: An Educational Manifesto*. New York: MacMillan, 1982.

Miner, Horace. "Body Ritual among the Nacirema." *American Anthropologist* 58.3 (1956): 503–07.

Roberts, Terry. *The Power of Paideia Schools: Defining Lives through Learning*. Alexandria: Association for Supervision and Curriculum Development, 1998.

Strong, Michael. *The Habit of Thought*. Chapel Hill, NC: New View, 1996.

4 Implementing Whole-Class Literature Discussions: An Overview of the Teacher's Roles

Sharon Eddleston
Robbinsdale Armstrong Senior High School,
Plymouth, Minnesota

Raymond A. Philippot
St. Cloud State University

Unfortunately, most schooling continues to be based on a transmission and recitation model of communication. Teachers talk and students listen. Applebee notes that his extensive literacy studies "reveal a continuing emphasis on learning about, rather than participating in, traditions of literature and criticism. . . . Most classrooms emphasized recitation rather than 'authentic' questions that encourage dialogue and debate" (29). If Rosenblatt is correct in arguing that the reader's or receiver's characteristics affect the way in which meaning is constructed from texts and messages (96–98), then the transmission model badly underestimates the activity of the receiver in making sense of a message. A new model for examining the dynamics of active participation in literature classrooms must be advanced if we are to move beyond traditional practices—a model that combines a constructivist approach to knowledge acquisition with rigorous literary analysis.

Developing an Environment for Classroom Discussion

Schools develop distinctive patterns of behavior, attitudes toward literacy, and beliefs about education and about the roles of teachers and students. Because these patterns are so institutionally ingrained, teachers interested in implementing whole-class discussions of literature in their classrooms ought to explain their rationale for doing so to their students. Additionally, teachers should aid their students in developing guidelines for these whole-class discussions.

To encourage students' diverse perspectives on literature, we recommend that teachers make explicit a reader-response based approach to analyzing meaning as presented in Beach's text *A Teacher's Introduction to Reader-Response Theories* and Probst's *Response and Analysis: Teaching Literature in Junior and Senior High School*. Furthermore, we urge teachers to discuss the value of a constructivist model of learning with their students. When we help them realize that they are active constructors of knowledge rather than passive recipients of information, students become more vested in the process. Sharon, for instance, begins each new semester at Robbinsdale Armstrong Senior High by discussing with her upper-level students her rationale for conducting whole-class discussions of literature and by reading excerpts from Probst's book on reader-response. She follows this up by modeling her own questions and observations about a work of fiction.

For example, in a recent discussion about Toni Morrison's novel *Beloved*, Sharon pointed to a passage about two turtles and indicated she didn't understand why this paragraph was included in the middle of the story. Mike, a senior in the class, said he thought there was a parallel between the turtles and the character Sethe, who closes herself off from others, while Paul D, a friend from Sethe's past, tries to draw her out of her shell. Mike's observation points out how, in whole-class discussions, teachers become students and students become teachers. When students are exposed to an English teacher modeling uncertain (i.e., tentative) interpretations of literature, they begin to see that fiction can be approached from numerous angles. Tentative explorations thus become the norm in the dialogic classroom.

Although speaking and responding to each other informally are common practices for most adolescents, such ease of conversation may stop when they are directed to generate academic talk centering on a particular novel. A variety of factors influence this phenomenon, including the following: a lack of experience in such settings, the size of the group, gender ratios, cultural diversity in the setting, social class, and other hidden tensions and conflicts within the classroom. Regardless of the reason for students' reluctance, we believe that an essential component of the language arts entails engaging students in discussion about literature. With that in mind, we offer the following strategies for helping students as they participate in whole-class literature discussions.

Multiple Roles of the Teacher

As students converse in literary discussions, they tend to question, agree and disagree, challenge, and help push one another's thinking along.

But they need to learn to do this. We can think of the teacher's role in whole-class discussion of literature as a collaborative one in which the instructor supports students' participation and helps them think ideas through. Recent studies of effective teaching have tried to capture this collaboration in metaphors such as "guiding," "mentoring," and "apprenticeship" (Rogoff 189–92).

Such metaphors emphasize the role of the teacher in providing support for the novice entering into a new domain. As one team of researchers describes it, the teacher's contributions provide students with "that needed bit of knowledge essential to achieving a further step" (Csikszentmihalyi, Rathunde, and Whalen 192), rather than seeking to ensure that they reach a particular endpoint. Questions, partial apprehensions, false starts, and new beginnings become part of the natural process of learning in this setting. When communication of this sort occurs and is supported in the English classroom, it aids in building a dialogic community where people expect to explore, argue, think, and learn.

The following discussion draws on Sharon's semester-long investigation of the dynamics of whole-class literature discussions at the aforementioned suburban Minneapolis high school, where she has taught for more than thirty years. Forty-eight college-bound juniors and seniors in two sections of Contemporary American Literature participated in large-group discussions of literature over four months. Sharon audiotaped the classes' talk about books and interviewed representative individuals about their experiences throughout the course. The study found that the teacher must take on a number of roles within the discussions if the conversations are to succeed. These roles include being a facilitator, a participant with ideas and questions, a promoter of diverse perspectives, a linker to real-world concerns, and an instructor of reading strategies. We briefly describe each role below.

Facilitator

We determined that extended stretches of linked conversation—often characterized by disagreements, alternative interpretations, and connections to discussants' real-world experiences—yield the greatest insights about the text under consideration. In the discussion setting, the teacher should be comfortable with "wait time," a period of silence between turns at talking. The facilitator should also remind students of previously agreed upon rules for classroom talk, such as not monopolizing time, refraining from put-downs, and allowing others the opportunity to speak without interruption. As facilitator, the teacher should also prod students to expand on their responses. For example, if a student says, "I think this character has a mental illness," the teacher, to help sharpen the student's insight, could respond, "Would you say more about what you're thinking?" or "What in the text leads you to believe that?" Probing questions such as these will press the student to elaborate on a response, as well as provoke other student reactions.

Participant with Ideas and Questions

Oftentimes a mismatch exists between the concerns and ideas an English teacher wants to discuss in a novel and what students deem interesting and important. This mismatch can be attributed largely to the teacher's more sophisticated approach to interpreting literature through years of practice, but it also derives from the fact that the teacher has most likely reread the text many times, while the students are first-time readers. The teacher should look for opportunities to raise his or her own questions or offer a tentative interpretation of a particularly confusing passage in an effort to expand student thinking.

For example, during a discussion of Michael Dorris's novel *Yellow Raft in Blue Water*, Sharon's students were exploring reasons why Christine, a teenager living on an American Indian reservation in Montana, was so eager to have her brother Lee enlist in the army. Sharon articulated the following response, which simultaneously modeled how to formulate a literary interpretation and provided insight into Christine's reasoning:

> There is a sense on the reservation, and this surprised me, that there's a real strong patriotism. Weren't you surprised at that? They talked about the powwows and how they'd always have a marching group that comes in, a drill corps or something. And the red, white, and blue, she [Christine] said, was a big thing on the reservation. And so partly she wants her brother to be patriotic so he can run for tribal offices. The guys who are running for tribal positions are veterans.

If the teacher, however, too often assumes an interpretive role, the students expect the "right answers" to come from the teacher, not themselves. In short, we recommend that the teacher refrain from doing too much of the students' work for them. Also, we urge the teacher to purchase as many class sets of new novels as the budget will allow, so that she or he, too, will be more of a first-time reader who must authentically struggle along with the students to make sense of an author's creation.

Promoter of Diverse Perspectives

We encourage teachers to pose open-ended questions that promote divergent thinking among students. Divergent thinking is often characterized by civil disagreement, and we have discovered that the more students are willing to engage in such disagreements about a text, the more focused and thoughtful they become about their reading. As students work to defend their positions more vigorously, they invariably resort to using textual evidence to help further their "cause." We are not suggesting that the discussion become a debate with winners and losers, but rather an open forum in which students test hypotheses and engage in alternative ways of thinking about literature.

Because literary works often depict instances of moral and ethical uncertainty, Sharon asks students to analyze and judge certain characters' motivations and actions. To accomplish this, she asks students to place characters on a moral continuum from despicable (1) to saintly (10). Students often view characters differently than teachers do, which in turn results in productive discussions. In one such case, Andrew, a senior in Sharon's class, gave the character Dayton (a good friend of Christine's brother Lee in *Yellow Raft in Blue Water*) a rating of 9 because Dayton rejected Christine's insincere sexual advances. Furthermore, Dayton refused to fight in the Vietnam war, a conflict he did not believe justifiable. April, another senior, concurred with Andrew's assessment, which prompted Matt, Burke, and Meggan to disagree, thus extending the conversation about the characters' motivations and behaviors. Also, this activity prepared the students to read on with a greater understanding of the characters' motivations.

Linker to Real-World Concerns

Students are often likely to frame their interpretations of literary works in terms of issues and problems related to their own real-world experiences and beliefs. Such connections allow students to view literature as valuable and applicable to their own lives. During the reading of Frank Chin's novel *Donald Duk*, several students expressed annoyance at the protagonist's twin sisters. Sharon encouraged a real-world link by stating the following: "Well, you know, this is set in California, and they almost sound like they're doing screen talk, doesn't it? Like it's movie talk. It's not natural conversation, it's very phony and kind of . . . they're being real clippy, sort of." Matt added that they seemed like "play-by-play announcers," which was followed by Stephanie's assertion that they came across like fairly normal sisters. Tim noted that the Duk family roles reminded him of a "first-born, second-born kind of thing."

> *Tim:*   I know in my family the second-born is usually the whiner and the one that's the baby. Sorry to all those second-borns out there. That's the way it seems to me in my family.

> *Michelle:*   Parents are a little bit lax after the first one. It always seems like things the first time are always a little more stressful.

These real-world connections not only help others understand a text better; they also lead students to reflect on their own real-life situations.

Instructor of Reading Strategies

When using the phrase "reading strategies," we are not referencing mechanistic and cognitive elements such as comprehension and decoding that are typically associated with reading instruction. Rather, we are talking about facility with literary concepts and devices found in high-quality novels and short stories. Of course we allow and encourage students' personal responses, but we also want to aid our students in examining the structural components of a work of literature so that they can take part in the process of critically examining it.

During one class period, Sharon's students expressed confusion regarding the point of view in *Donald Duk*. Seizing this teachable moment, Sharon stated:

> That's called "third person limited." When you're in the mind of one character. We don't get into Arnold's mind, right? It's only when Arnold says something that we know what he's thinking. So this is all sort of stream-of-consciousness through Donald's point of view. That's called third person limited. If we get into the minds of many characters, then it would be third person omniscient.

Sharon's offering of this knowledge helped the students not only increase their general understanding of how authors construct fictional works through the use of literary devices, but also further their understanding of the particular novel under discussion.

Support Strategies to Encourage Classroom Talk

In addition to assuming a number of roles when leading whole-class discussions, teachers must determine the text selections, related writing activities, and assessment strategies that will best support the discussions.

Text Selection

This is a key factor in stimulating whole-class discussions of literature. Generally speaking, the more interesting the students find a book, the more likely they are to want to talk about it. However, Sharon offers a number of diverse works that students may not always find immediately accessible, and the lack of familiarity with these works tends to generate valuable talk. Several of the books and plays that Sharon has found to be successful include *Fences* by August Wilson, *In the Lake of the Woods* by Tim O'Brien, *A Gathering of Old Men* by Ernest J. Gaines, and *Death and the Maiden* by Ariel Dorfman. Novels containing controversial elements also tend to evoke lively discussion. F. Scott Fitzgerald's *The Great Gatsby*, for example, offers an array of themes and actions that students find engaging, from Gatsby's shady background and dubiously acquired wealth, to murder and deceit. We are by no means advocating only the use of texts that are in one way or another controversial; however, we do claim that the more easily understood the reading material, the less dynamic the ensuing discussion. We believe that the strategies outlined in this article can be used with almost any text, though we advocate books that are intellectually accessible even as they require a great deal of critical insight on the part of young readers.

Writing to Learn

Another aspect teachers must attend to if they are to support whole-class literature discussions is developing complementary writing-to-learn strategies. For the less vocal students in Sharon's classes, feeling unprepared to speak inhibited their participation. However, through a series of writing activities, such as the ones discussed below, teachers can help both extroverted and introverted students prepare to engage in more thoughtful, provocative literature discussions.

"Shortwrites"

These pieces promote thinking about a particular issue or topic in a confined amount of space and time (students write no more than three sentences in seven minutes). Ideally, shortwrites should allow for divergent thinking among the participants while at the same time act as a reading check. For example, Sharon asked her students, who were in the early stages of reading Barbara Kingsolver's *The Bean Trees*, to respond to the following prompt: "In no more than three sentences, explain why Taylor keeps the baby she has been given. Include at least three specifics from the text in your answer." The responses students wrote allowed the class to use their answers as a jumping-off point for the discussion. Below is the start of the discussion based on the prompt:

Matt: It seems like she just took it and that was it. She didn't put up a fight, and I mean, what if a woman got into my car and said, 'Here, here, take this baby'? First off, I'd think she was nuts for getting into my car. Secondly, I don't think I'd take the baby because I mean that's just something you don't get handed. That's a life. That's something that's, it's dependent on you, and if you don't take care of it, then you're going to have problems.

April: Maybe she felt sorry for the older lady that had the baby in the first place.

John: I mean, that's why she escaped. That's why she left. She's one of the few survivors that made it out of there [her home town] without actually getting pregnant, and it seems like now she's being handed one, and that just doesn't fit together, I don't think.

Jay: Well, it seems like she didn't really have a choice because she was kind of confused, and she was kind of scared. So maybe if she takes it to the police, she'll get in trouble for having it. So I think she's kind of scared.

In this exchange students collaboratively search for an interpretive understanding of the text in question. Additionally, they tentatively search for character motivation, realizing that a definitive answer may not exist. The shortwrite preceding this exchange had provided students with necessary "rehearsal" time to formulate insightful commentary, which traditional approaches to literary discussion don't often permit.

Journaling

This is another writing-to-learn strategy that sets the stage for participating in whole-class discussions. By telling students that a reading journal is particularly well-suited to helping them explore especially interesting, confusing, or controversial aspects of a text, teachers prepare the discussants to question texts in ways they might not otherwise feel comfortable doing. The reading journal also lays the groundwork for students to speak in front of others with tentative interpretations. In short, a journal serves as another "rehearsal" space for students to explore or entertain ideas related to a text in an unthreatening environment. These ideas can then be used as seeds for contributions to the whole-class discussion.

Inquiry Papers

Teachers can also spur whole-class discussion through the use of inquiry papers. While reading and discussing Frank Chin's novel *Donald Duk*, the students in Sharon's class prepared papers that addressed a self-selected question they had about a section of the text. On a given discussion day, three or four students presented their papers, the content of which had to include the question to be addressed and a minimum of three possible answers to the question, all requiring text-based support. At the beginning of class, the presenters wrote their questions on the chalkboard, and the class discussed each question before reading the writer's paper, copies of which were given to all participants. Students broached various topics, including the following: Why does Donald burn the plane early in the story? Why is he able to dream historical dreams about events he knows nothing about? Why does the character called "American Cong" have a part in the story? Why does Frank Chin write the way he does? Why does he end the book so abruptly? When students determine the focus and direction of classroom talk, such as they do in inquiry papers, they participate more willingly, thus making for rich, authentic discussion.

Assessment

As parents, administrators, and politicians increasingly call for accountability in the classroom, we would be remiss if we ignored the challenging task of assessing classroom talk. We suggest two primary forms of accountability. First, teachers should tally who speaks and how often. Such a practice may seem overwhelming and messy at first, but we have found that it is well worth the effort to establish a system to keep students aware of their contributions to the discussions. In addition—and, we think, more important—informing students about their participation helps them become proficient self-assessors of their contributions to the discussions. Toward this end, Sharon created a discussion rubric that students use to evaluate their roles in the discussions throughout the semester. The rubric reads as follows:

Name: _____

Discussion Rubric

5

This discussant accepts responsibility for making meaning out of literature. He/she consistently demonstrates a careful reading of the text and makes insightful comments that significantly contribute to our understanding of a reading. The discussant refers to specifics from the class text, compares and contrasts that text with related texts, and makes connections with personal experiences and social and cultural issues. A respectful listener who avoids monopolizing the conversation, he/she sometimes pulls together and reflects on ideas that have surfaced in the inquiry discussions and may also ask relevant follow-up questions, thereby pulling other students into the discussion.

4

Although speaking less frequently than the discussant described above, this discussant shows growth in willingness to express responses. He/she has the ability to explain ideas clearly and to connect those ideas to others being discussed. This discussant may clarify a specific point being discussed or elaborate on specific examples from the text. Body language and eye contact also indicate substantial involvement in the discussion.

3

Speaking occasionally, this discussant may primarily respond on a personal level to the text ("I like it," or "I didn't like it"), perhaps supplying some textual evidence for this point of view. The discussant's remarks may be insightful but they tend to be brief. Or, the discussant may speak often but says little that adds significantly to our understanding of a text, and may, in fact, primarily repeat what others have already said or be difficult to follow.

2

This class member says little. This discussant's few remarks may be inaccurate, unclear, or too brief to be helpful. Little textual support is offered; there is little evidence that the student has read the text carefully or at all. Or, the student may belittle other speakers' remarks, monopolize the conversation, interrupt other speakers, ignore their remarks when speaking, or talk to those seated nearby rather than to the whole group.

1

The student says nothing and appears uninterested in the class discussions. Or, the student may appear interested in the discussions but, for whatever reason, does not join in.

At the bottom of the rubric form, each student also assesses the class's discussion abilities in terms of what it does well and what it needs to improve upon. Thus, beyond merely assigning grades to students, the assessment process provides students with feedback about their progress in the discussion setting as well as opportunities to evaluate themselves and the class as a whole, and it gives teachers information about participation patterns, group trends, and gender roles in this forum.

Conclusion

Teachers should assume diverse roles in whole-class discussions of literature if they expect to foster fruitful conversations. Establishing a system that allows students to participate in whole-class discussions is no easy feat; in fact, immediate success, in our experiences, may not occur. Therefore, we urge those who want to use this method of inquiry to exercise patience and fortitude.

In taking on these various roles, the teacher aids students in (1) voicing their own ideas, (2) hearing others in ways that push their own thinking, (3) becoming sensitive to viewpoints that differ from their own, (4) thinking deeply, and (5) communicating clearly. Through text selection, development of written assignments, and implementation of various assessment strategies, teachers help support whole-class discussions of literature in crucial ways.

Works Cited

Applebee, Arthur N. *Curriculum as Conversation: Transforming Traditions of Teaching and Learning.* Chicago: U of Chicago P, 1996.

Beach, Richard W. *A Teacher's Introduction to Reader-Response Theories.* Urbana, IL: NCTE, 1993.

Csikszentmihalyi, Mihaly, Kevin Rathunde, and Samuel Whalen. *Talented Teenagers: The Roots of Success and Failure.* New York: Cambridge UP, 1993.

Probst, Robert E. *Response and Analysis: Teaching Literature in Junior and Senior High School.* Portsmouth, NH: Boynton/Cook, 1988.

Rogoff, Barbara. *Apprenticeship in Thinking: Cognitive Development in Social Context.* New York: Oxford UP, 1990.

Rosenblatt, Louise M. *Literature as Exploration.* New York: D. Appleton-Century, 1938.

5 Whose Inquiry Is It Anyway? Using Students' Questions in the Teaching of Literature

G. Douglas Meyers
University of Texas at El Paso

One way of describing so-called growing up would be to say that it involves a transition from the imperative to the interrogative; from Food!—*through* I want—*to* Can I have? *Questions are, among other things, the grammatical form we give to our desire. . . . If questioning is a way of desiring, answering must be akin to satisfying; a meeting of desire. . . . To learn to question, and to learn not to, are the basic building blocks of development. To know just what can be questioned and what must not be—and to learn . . . what constitutes a question—is what education educates us for. . . . What would we be able to do together—what would we be able to say—if interrogation were banned?*

Adam Phillips, "An Answer to Questions"

These speculations by Adam Phillips at the start of the new century provide a provocative context for considering that not enough attention has been paid to the use of student-generated questions in class discussions of literary works. Much excellent work has been devoted to the role of teacher questioning in discussions (see Hynds for a fine review), but proportionally little has appeared about students' questions. Though their use in journals (e.g., Biddle and Fulwiler 20), portfolios (e.g., Purves and Quattrini), and letters exchanged between students (e.g., Fishman and McCarthy 107) has been detailed, the critical role of student-generated questions in classroom discussions of literature is a topic that has been largely underplayed (excepting Corcoran and Monseau). This is surprising, given the prominent position discussion now holds as a methodology for teaching literature and given the high value we claim for inquiry approaches and active learning.

The life of a literary work germinates when a reader encounters words on a page. We know that literary reading involves some sort of aesthetic and creative response on the part of the reader, and constructivists often use the word "transaction" to describe the act of reading, making the dialogic relationship between reader and text preeminent (Rosenblatt; Purves, Rogers, and Soter). In this article I would like to extend that transaction to include the interactions that can happen after a reader has read the last word on the page, and I would also like to extend that dialogue to consider what teachers can do to sustain conversation after reading and transport it to the larger domain of classroom discussion.

Genuine dialogue rarely results when one privileged person gets to ask all of the questions while everyone else simply answers, deprived of the chance to articulate questions of their own. Whose inquiry is that, anyway? Is it even fair to call it inquiry? Don't we really believe that authentic inquiry starts by determining and exploring one's own questions? If that's the case, then it should be easy to see the value of replacing teacher-directed questioning in discussions of literature with student-generated questioning (or at least subordinating the teacher-directed to the student-generated), if the discussions are to be truly inquiry-based.

In this article I will discuss ten ways of involving students in creating questions to be used in the discussion of literature. Such discussion can be either small-group or whole-class. My focus is less on the discussions themselves and more on the process of students' generating questions in writing before their discussions, setting in motion a teaching-learning scenario whereby each individual routinely brings his or her questions to the discussion, shares them, and has them answered by others participating in the discussion. Such an approach facilitates what the recent research in literary instruction (e.g., Applebee, Burroughs, and Stevens) describes as curricular coherence and continuity, possessing as it does a structure that promotes attention to related ideas over extended periods of time coupled with conventions for students' participation.

The epistemological assumption underlying the paramount role of student-generated questions in class discussions is that expressed so well by Mayher: "There is no knowledge without a knower. . . . Human beings are active meaning makers who are continually learning—making personal knowledge—when they can act according to their own purposes" (79). *To their own purposes*: each reader of each work of literature, as Langer notes, is "reaching toward a horizon of possibilities," possibilities of understanding which cohere and develop as "envisionments"—unique sets of ideas, images, and questions about the literary work ("Rethinking" 37–39). It is out of such envisionments, out of their own purposes, that students are motivated to generate and explore questions, for only from that wellspring of curiosity can questions fully embody the growth and desire Phillips mentions in the opening quotation.

In addition to such cognitive benefits, discussions inspired by student-generated questions also yield good results for classroom dynamics. When a teacher institutionalizes student questioning as a crucial part of classroom discourse, real authority is given to students' voices, for they are helping to determine what it is legitimate to talk about. In a democratic society, as Pradl argues, the importance of such classroom ecology is anything but trivial, and it can certainly contribute to a classroom's being galvanized by the "collectivist" energy Hurlbert describes. What is learned, we know, is in part a function of how it is learned; and in my experience, my college students' anticipation of, participation in, and reflection about creating, sharing, and discussing their own questions after they read a work of literature enrich and deepen the literary experience for them and contribute significantly to their growth as responsive and responsible readers.

The following ten activities focus on a variety of ways in which students can write questions about works of literature in preparation to discuss them. Just as there is no single reading skill suited to every type of text (Beach and Appleman 115), there is no single questioning skill that can be applied with equal success to all literary works. The one thing that all ten activities have in common is that they do not involve students in answering their own questions, for I have discovered that when students are not encumbered by the need to provide answers, their questions grow in importance, interest, and complexity.

Space limitations prohibit including the number and variety of examples of students' questions that I would have liked, but I would be pleased to share additional illustrative student work with individuals who request it.

1. Creating One Key Question about a Literary Work

Each student generates one question that he or she believes is important and thought-provoking. The advantage of this activity is that it enables students to inquire unselfconsciously and freely into a work of literature from any angle that appeals to them. It sensitizes them to something in which they are authentically interested and in so doing promotes the empowered position of being a "situated reader" (Vine and Faust 107) whose ownership of the literary work grows out of her or his particular question. There are other advantages to this simple activity: because (unlike as with answers) there is no such thing as a wrong question, students are successful from the start; because it is a single question that is asked, students must often distill their ideas in ways that require the concentration of "thoughtful readers" (Pearson and Tierney 144); and because many students make the effort to pose a question so original that no one else will ask it, creativity is encouraged. When the same question does recur in several responses, however, it provides a teachable moment for investigating something at the heart of the literary work.

2. Creating One Key Question and Explaining Its Importance

This activity ups the ante on the first, adding to it some reflective commentary. By helping students to become more aware of the issues that are embedded in their question by explaining its importance, this activity deepens their understanding of the literary work and their response to it. As with the first activity, students are guaranteed success because there is no way to do this wrong.

3. Creating a List of Important Questions about a Literary Work

Though it takes more time than the first two activities, creating a list of questions may in some ways be easier because students are released from any pressure to write a single "best" question. This activity gives students the freedom to range among the unlimited interests they may have in a work of literature (and its context) without having to articulate why they have them. It also provides students the opportunity to mull over, if only unconsciously, how their various questions might coalesce; that is, what, if any, commonalities inhere in them? This activity generates a certain exuberance in students because of the special kind of energy associated with creating five or six questions (the number I generally ask students to write) entirely of their own choosing.

4. Creating a List of Important Questions and Rank-Ordering Them

This activity builds on the previous one by having students create a list of questions and then reflect on their questions enough so that they can rank-order them from, say, most important to least important, or best to worst, or most interesting to least interesting (the variable for rank-ing can change according to the students' desire). An activity that Ander-son and Rubano rightfully say "guarantees an aesthetic response" (36), rank-ordering questions taps students' tacit knowledge about literature in a way that does not make them defensive about the appropriateness of their ranking; it is simply done, not explained. (This activity, by the way, has interesting links to research assessing students' achievement in literature conducted in the 1970s by the International Association for the Evaluation of Educational Achievement, in which Purves found both similarities and differences between students from different countries in terms of the questions they preferred and rejected.)

5. Creating a List of Important Questions and Rank-Ordering Them—with an Explanation

Analogous to the progression between activities 1 and 2, the progres-sion between activities 4 and 5 involves preparing reflective commen-tary—in this case an articulation of the rationale and criteria for rank-ordering questions, which is an activity that generates significant critical thinking. To explain why one question is better than another (or more important, or more interesting, etc.) involves sharpening one's ability to make literary judgments as well as one's ability to argue them.

These five question-generating activities have proven to be powerful modes of inquiry in my literature classes. Using them, students have created hundreds of questions; I have learned a great deal from our dis-cussions of them, and students have learned a great deal from one an-other and from themselves. Though these activities and the discussions that follow are by no means "anything goes" free-for-alls, they certainly set in motion something that cannot be fully controlled or predicted by the teacher. When I first started employing them, it required some re-straint on my part to merely *accept* students' questions (and their com-mentaries about them, when required) rather than to use them didacti-cally as examples to illustrate my predetermined points. I mention this by way of acknowledging a natural reluctance many teachers may have about letting students inquire so freely, and to suggest that David Bleich's observation related to this matter may be instructive:

> If we acquire the courage to eschew our patronizing task of "in-troducing" students to "our" style of study, and instead ask all our students, younger or older, to introduce their own ways and thoughts for mutual sharing, we will have begun a productive

response to the many voices now seeking to educate for an authentically just society. (21–22)

It is nonetheless undeniable that as literature teachers we know more than our students about which kinds of questions about literary works might bear the best fruit. This expertise is one of our greatest assets, one that should be shared with students. Following Applebee, if our students are relative novices in the field of literary study, then it makes sense that they "learn the knowledge-in-action [i.e., the tacit knowledge] out of which the field is constituted" (11). Providing students with heuristics for posing questions about literature—"knowledge-in-action"—can thus be a strategic way to broaden their knowledge of our field's traditional disciplinary conventions. The following five question-generating activities, more structured than the first five but still entirely dependent upon students' making them their own by adapting them to their own purposes, are ones that I have used to do just that. Not inert sets of rules, they are active meaning-making processes that expand students' repertoires of question-generating skills.

6. Creating Questions Based on Purves and Rippere's Four Categories of Response

Among the earliest detailed analyses that classified types of student response to literary works was Purves and Rippere's 1968 NCTE monograph in which they propose four basic response categories:

- engagement-involvement (E-I),
- perception (P),
- interpretation (I), and
- evaluation (E).

Intended to be neither exhaustive nor taxonomical, these four categories can provide students with one model (and the vocabulary associated with it) for examining their own responses to literary works and constructing questions which deliberately sample each area. Engagement-response questions inquire about personal reactions to and re-creations of the literary work; perception questions deal with the analysis of its literary and rhetorical devices and structure; interpretation questions seek to uncover meaning in the work, often through inference and generalization; and evaluation questions ask for judgments about the work. The following questions, generated by students after reading Sandra Cisneros's collection of short stories *The House on Mango Street*,

originate in Purves and Rippere's system and are typical of those created using this model:

(E-I)   In what ways did reading these stories make you think
        of your own neighborhood when you were growing up?

(P)   How do similes contribute to the style of these stories?

(I)   How is the narrator's name [Esperanza] related to the
        theme of *The House on Mango Street?*

(E)   What is the best story in this collection? Why?

7. Creating a Set of Questions Focused on Literary Elements

Depending on the genre under study and the level of development of
the students, the literary elements on which discussion focuses will
change, as will the degree of emphasis placed on them. In an introductory college literature course devoted primarily to fiction, for instance,
I use seven elements of fiction—character, plot, point of view, setting,
style, symbolism, and theme—as a springboard for students to construct
seven different questions about novels and short stories. Among the
chief benefits of anchoring questions in these literary elements is that it
makes the elements into tools that each reader can internalize to ask his
or her own questions about a work of literature, rather than mere textbook terms whose definitions are mindlessly regurgitated with little
relevance to one's own purposes. Students generally enjoy writing questions based on the literary elements because this activity facilitates
making both the literary work and the literary elements their own.

8. Creating a Set of Questions Based on the Questioning Circle

Christenbury and Kelly's Questioning Circle (discussed in Simmons and
Deluzain 150–51) is based on the idea that there are three basic kinds of
questions that spring from reading a work of literature:

- questions about the reader (R),
- questions about the text (T), and
- questions about the world, including other literature (W).

While each type—each "circle"—of question is independent of the others, intersections between one circle and the others do occur, generating three additional types of questions, "shaded" questions:

- questions about the text and the reader (T-R),

- questions about the text and the world (T-W), and
- questions about the reader and the world (R-W).

Finally, there is an area where all three circles overlap, generating a seventh kind of question, one the authors call a "dense" one:

- questions about the text, the reader, and the world (T-R-W).

As was the case with the Purves and Rippere response categories in activity 6, students can adapt this model for the purpose of generating questions. Given the complicated kinds of thinking it prompts, the Questioning Circle enhances the sophistication of students' questions as well as their language for describing and understanding those questions.

The following questions about *The House on Mango Street* were generated by students using the Questioning Circle model:

(R)	What does the word "home" mean to you?
(T)	Why did Esperanza's mother drop out of school?
(W)	What things make up a person's "roots"?
(T-R)	Which character were you most affected by? Why?
(T-W)	How are the issues facing the female characters in many of these stories, which were published in 1984, relevant to our world today?
(R-W)	How do you think childhood environment influences the kind of person one grows up to be?
(T-R-W)	How would you expect most people to deal with the kinds of problems that Sally faced? Why? Would their way of responding be better or worse than hers? Why?

Since the Questioning Circle model defines "the world" to include other works of literature, it also affords the opportunity for students to create questions that make comparisons between different literary works. Because one of the characteristics of maturation as a reader of literature is an awareness that every text is related to other texts, questions of this synthetic nature are especially important as they engage students in inquiry about the multiple horizons of possibilities that become visible when they explore more than one literary landscape at a time.

Related to the Questioning Circle, but involving a simpler scale, is the model proposed by Schilb, wherein students probe a literary work using the foci of text, reader, author, and history.

9. Creating a Set of Questions Focused on Literal and Inferential Levels of Questions

In *Writing about Literature*, Kahn, Walter, and Johannessen note seven basic types of text-based questions that might be asked of a literary work (5). At the literal level of comprehension, there are questions about

- basic stated information (SI),
- key details (KD), and
- stated relationships (SR).

At the inferential level of comprehension, we find questions about

- simple implied relationships (SIR),
- complex implied relationships (CIR),
- authors' generalizations (AG), and
- structural generalizations (SG).

Again, as this last set of questions about *The House on Mango Street* illustrates, students may be taught this model as a means for generating questions about a literary work:

(SI)   What does the narrator say her name means in Spanish and in English?

(KD)   What is growing in front of the house on Mango Street?

(SR)   Why does the old lady in "The Three Sisters" use the image of the circle when talking to Esperanza?

(SIR)   How do Esperanza's feelings about her father compare with his feelings about his father?

(CIR)   What were Sally's reasons for getting married so young?

(AG)   What is Cisneros saying about the role of literacy in the process of self-actualization?

(SG)   What effect does the order of these stories have on the way we understand the development of Esperanza?

10. Creating Questions Based on Particular Critical Approaches

If one of the teacher's goals is to engage students in literary inquiry from a particular critical perspective, students can be asked to generate questions using that critical approach. Related to this activity is Blake's model of a "'critical' reader response" to literature that involves readers' assuming a certain ideology or stance and examining a literary work's assumptions and perspectives about matters such as gender, race, and class.

While I have emphasized the usefulness of students' generating questions prior to class discussion, questioning is not a linear process, and employing these activities recursively is therefore natural and desirable. Students can learn a great deal when they also create questions after class discussions, especially since discussions seldom result in consensus and therefore can easily propel further questioning and, to return to Langer's term, envisionment-building. Having each student write yet another question is a productive way to spend five minutes at the end of a class discussion, for it provides closure on the current discussion and an entree into the next one. What matters is that the questions be *students' authentic questions*, ones from which they will derive satisfaction in creating and considering in a classroom that celebrates diverse ways of interrogating works of literature.

Knowing how to ask questions inspires lifelong learning. Knowing how to ask questions about literature empowers lifelong reading, the promotion of which, I believe, should be our ultimate goal as literature teachers. "Literature," Langer reminds us, "makes us better thinkers. It moves us to see the multi-sidedness of situations and therefore expands the breadth of our own visions, moving us toward dreams and solutions we might not otherwise have imagined. . . . [I]t moves us to consider our interconnectedness with others and the intrinsic pluralism of meaning; it helps us become more human" (*Envisioning* 145). In the passage quoted at the beginning of this article, Phillips wonders, "What would we be able to do together—what would we be able to say—if interrogation were banned?" I would like to conclude by imagining just the opposite. If interrogation were *required*, if we treated students' questions as a critical part of their literary instruction, if every student from kindergarten through college were required to write original questions to share in classroom discussions of literature, what would we *not* be able to do together, as learners and citizens? Until that day comes, we need to keep asking: Whose inquiry is it anyway?

Works Cited

Anderson, Philip M., and Gregory Rubano. *Enhancing Aesthetic Reading and Response*. Urbana, IL: NCTE, 1991.

Applebee, Arthur N. *Curriculum as Conversation: Transforming Traditions of Teaching and Learning*. Chicago: University of Chicago Press, 1996.

Applebee, Arthur N., Robert Burroughs, and Anita S. Stevens. "Creating Continuity and Coherence in High School Literature Curricula." *Research in the Teaching of English* 34.4 (2000): 396–429.

Beach, Richard, and Deborah Appleman. "Reading Strategies for Expository and Literary Text Types." *Becoming Readers in a Complex Society.* Ed. Alan C. Purves and Olive Niles. Chicago: The National Society for the Study of Education, 1984. 115–43.

Biddle, Arthur W., and Toby Fulwiler. *Reading, Writing, and the Study of Literature.* New York: Random, 1989.

Blake, Brett Elizabeth. "'Critical' Reader Response in an Urban Classroom: Creating Cultural Texts to Engage Diverse Readers." *Theory into Practice* 37.3 (1998): 238–43.

Bleich, David. "Reading from Inside and Outside of One's Community." *Practicing Theory in Introductory College Literature Courses.* Ed. James M. Cahalan and David B. Downing. Urbana, IL: NCTE, 1991. 19–35.

Cisneros, Sandra. *The House on Mango Street.* Houston: Arte Publico, 1984.

Corcoran, Bill. "Teachers Creating Readers." *Readers, Texts, Teachers.* Ed. Bill Corcoran and Emrys Evans. Upper Montclair, NJ: Boynton/Cook, 1987. 41–74.

Fishman, Stephen M., and Lucille McCarthy. *John Dewey and the Challenge of Classroom Practice.* New York: Teachers College Press; and Urbana, IL: NCTE, 1998.

Hurlbert, C. Mark. "The Walls We Don't See: Toward Collectivist Pedagogies as Political Struggle." *Practicing Theory in Introductory College Literature Courses.* Ed. James M. Cahalan and David B. Downing. Urbana, IL: NCTE, 1991. 131–48.

Hynds, Susan. "Challenging Questions in the Teaching of Literature." *Literature Instruction: A Focus on Student Response.* Ed. Judith A. Langer. Urbana, IL: NCTE, 1992. 78–100.

Kahn, Elizabeth A., Carolyn Calhoun Walter, and Larry R. Johannessen. *Writing about Literature.* Urbana, IL: NCTE, 1984.

Langer, Judith A. *Envisioning Literature: Literary Understanding and Literature Instruction.* New York: Teachers College Press, 1995.

———. "Rethinking Literature Instruction." *Literature Instruction: A Focus on Student Response.* Ed. Judith A. Langer. Urbana, IL: NCTE, 1992. 35–53.

Mayher, John S. *Uncommon Sense: Theoretical Practice in Language Education.* Portsmouth, NH: Boynton/Cook, 1990.

Monseau, Virginia R. "Students and Teachers as a Community of Readers." *Reading Their World: The Young Adult Novel in the Classroom.* Ed. Virginia R. Monseau and Gary M. Salvner. Portsmouth, NH: Boynton/Cook, 1992. 85–98.

Pearson, P. David, and Robert J. Tierney. "On Becoming a Thoughtful Reader: Learning to Read Like a Writer." *Becoming Readers in a Complex Society.* Ed. Alan C. Purves and Olive Niles. Chicago: The National Society for the Study of Education, 1984. 144–173.

Phillips, Adam. "An Answer to Questions." *The Threepenny Review* 81 (2000): 6.

Pradl, Gordon M. *Literature for Democracy: Reading as a Social Act.* Portsmouth, NH: Boynton/Cook, 1996.

Purves, Alan C. *Reading and Literature: American Achievement in International Perspective.* Urbana, IL: NCTE, 1981.

Purves, Alan C., and Joseph A. Quattrini. *Creating the Literature Portfolio: A Guide for Students.* Lincolnwood, IL: NTC, 1997.

Purves, Alan C., and Victoria Rippere. *Elements of Writing about a Literary Work: A Study of Response to Literature.* Urbana, IL: NCTE, 1968.

Purves, Alan C., Theresa Rogers, and Anna O. Soter. *How Porcupines Make Love II: Teaching a Response-Centered Literature Curriculum.* New York: Longman, 1990.

Rosenblatt, Louise M. *Literature as Exploration.* 5th ed. New York: MLA, 1995.

Schilb, John. "'Text,' 'Reader,' 'Author,' and 'History' in the Introduction to Literature Course." *Practicing Theory in Introductory College Literature Courses.* Ed. James M. Cahalan and David B. Downing. Urbana, IL: NCTE, 1991. 59–71.

Simmons, John S., and H. Edward Deluzain. *Teaching Literature in Middle and Secondary Grades.* Boston: Allyn and Bacon, 1992.

Vine, Harold A., Jr., and Mark A. Faust. *Situating Readers: Students Making Meaning of Literature.* Urbana, IL: NCTE, 1993.

6 Different Questions, Bigger Answers: Matching the Scope of Inquiry to Students' Needs

John S. Schmit
Augsburg College

An encounter with a text like Ralph Ellison's "The Battle Royal" quickly has the reader asking questions. What is it like to know the kind of brutality and prejudice that the story describes? How do we cope with the horror we feel after reading this story? And what does it mean to "live with your head in the lion's mouth"? When we read a text like "The Battle Royal," we share these questions and others; but making our way to answers requires as much method as thought. As teachers we wonder where the discussion of such a text should start.

We might start by asking what questions the literary text poses. Building a class discussion around a series of questions is nothing new. Recently, though, the nature of the questions that teachers ask has shifted from "What am I thinking?" to "What are you thinking?" Inquiry-based learning has put a new face on the interrogation of literature. In a sense, too, the object of interrogation has changed, since literary texts are now seen as territories for exploration. If we want to map them accurately, though, we need to cover ground systematically, even in spite of our excitement to find treasures—the answers to our really big questions.

As we plan student discussions of challenging literary texts, we need to assess the abilities and needs of our students. Do they have sufficient historical background to comprehend the context of the piece? Have they previously read works of the same genre? Are they aware of social issues or cultural constraints in their own world with which they can make connections in order to see the relevance of the text? In general, what do they need to know or review before they will be ready to move into an exploration of the meaning of the text? Any plan for textual investigation must move forward from an accounting of student needs.

Older models of classroom interrogation required students to follow the leader. For example, at the heart of the old Socratic method lay a series of questions, carefully posed to help students get at some truth, some especially important idea. When this method is practiced in its more traditional forms, the path to a desired truth has already been carefully mapped. The person who asks the questions has already decided on the discussion's destination. Traditional Socratic questions, for the most part, are closed-ended; there are correct and incorrect answers. Correct answers proceed along the road toward a single predetermined truth, while incorrect answers threaten to take the learner into a wilderness of confusion.

More often than not, these days, traditional Socratic seminars have been replaced by forms of classroom inquiry that revolve around open-ended questions: questions that do not elicit responses that one would call "correct" or "incorrect." In an appropriately postcolonial way, the objective of open-ended inquiry is exploration rather than discovery. Open ended discussions give students the latitude they need in order to search. In the interpretation of literature, for example, the teacher's questions can direct students to an important area of the text and then allow them to find what truths they can. While students may hold their own interpretations, within the framework of large-group inquiry, these truths are truths of agreement—pared and shaped by discussion rather than specified by the instructor's questions.

When teachers employ open-ended inquiry in the classroom, they demonstrate that questions are motives rather than imperatives; they are reasons for looking at the text again. Too frequently in the past, classroom questions were perceived by students as commands to present an answer rather than invitations to find one. In the largest sense, questions are representations of what we need or desire to know; they provide a framework for the examination of ideas. Closed-ended questions help the teacher set a context for open-ended inquiry, which follows constructivist principles. Open-ended inquiry places responsibility for investigation in the students' hands. Readers are free to leave the well-paved path of traditional Socratic inquiry and begin their careers as textual cartographers. Working cooperatively, they are able to map the landscape of each text they encounter.

Open-Ended versus Closed-Ended Questions

As we think about the needs our students have in order to understand a literary work, many of us worry about what will happen if the preparations for their exploration come up short. Sometimes images of disastrous expeditions loom in our imaginations, and none of us wants to send off an ill-equipped explorer who, like Robert Falcon Scott, will be unable to return alive from some metaphorical South Pole. "How soon," the teacher might ask then, "is it appropriate for me to let my students explore interpretive landscapes on their own?" After all, responsible teaching entails concern for the intellectual safety of students setting about the task of inquiry. If the teacher deems it necessary, she or he can prepare the students through discussion in a more controlled setting. Within Mortimer J. Adler's Paideia framework, for example, seminar leaders will typically differentiate the kinds of books that they are teaching, and they will ask different kinds of questions based on the kind of book they have at hand. Speaking on the conduct of seminars, Adler and Charles Van Doren remark that "[a] seminar about Shakespeare's *Hamlet*, for example, is different from a seminar about Aristotle's *Ethics*. An able seminar leader conducts the two seminars in different ways" (Adler and Van Doren 19–20). Explorations of imaginative literature will necessarily seem more chaotic and less orderly than explorations of expository literature, which will tend to be more linear and factual.

Another way to characterize such pedagogical differences is to make distinctions between "open" and "tutorial" seminars. Open seminars focus to a greater extent on open-ended questions and issues of interpretation, while tutorial seminars center on more factual information about the text at hand and are likely to employ a greater number of questions for which the answer might be a simple "yes" or "no." For example, regarding Ralph Ellison's "The Battle Royal," one might first ask students a question like "What is a 'smoker'?" The answer to this question is evident and researchable. This question might be followed by one inviting more discursive responses: "Why does Ellison choose to set the action of his first chapter at a smoker?" When we ask open-ended questions, in a sense we simply issue passports to our students, allowing them to travel where they will; tutorial seminars, on the other hand, resemble guided tours. The teacher can choose between the two depending on the text under consideration, as well as the abilities and knowledge of the student population.

Tutorial or "closed" seminars can be used to promote greater comprehension of a text where the goal of the seminar is to provide clarity and common understanding. For example, teachers typically want to ensure that students know what a challenging text says before moving on to a discussion of what that text means. Also, by posing simpler, more pointed questions, teachers may foster students' confidence and assure familiarity with necessary background information. The "closed" seminar provides an overview of the territory before the journey itself takes place. The "tutorial" seminar, then, is precursory. It provides a prefatory description of the landscape to be mapped, and the teacher takes on the role of the responsible guide, the one who warns of the places beyond which lie dragons.

Once students have demonstrated readiness to explore a text, the focus of inquiry can shift to more open-ended discussion. The discussion leader can pose questions that have a wider variety of possible answers, and the participants in these seminars can construct their own individual and collective truths and thus form their own interpretations.

Another strength of the model that Adler developed for Paideia is that the seminars are student-focused. The learning process of the "open" seminar involves the invention of new ideas. The rules also reflect a collaborative purpose. Participants are coached to speak directly to each other and not to address their remarks to the seminar leader. They are taught to regulate their own responses, speaking when others are not speaking, and they are free to negotiate their conclusions through agreement and disagreement. Negotiation of truth is possible because the question, not the teacher, regulates the conversation.

Some Illustrations of Closed- and Open-Ended Questions in Practice

The discussion that follows requires a caveat. The model outlined here is intended for illustration. Like a model airplane, I hope, it will provide a likeness of the real thing in miniature, but one should think twice before picking it up and attempting to float it across the room. It is not intended as a substitute for the real planning of a classroom discussion. This model, for example, is linear in ways that classroom discussions assuredly are not. Still, I hope that it is useful for its intended purpose.

Consider again a discussion of Ellison's "The Battle Royal." Because this story is also the first chapter of one of America's greatest novels, *Invisible Man*, it deserves careful attention. It is also rich in interpretive possibilities, and, as I have suggested, it elicits a variety of difficult questions right from the outset. To structure a discussion of this piece in a way that will move toward these initial questions, a teacher might elect to sharpen students' focus on the text by first posing a series of closed-ended questions.

Closed-Ended Questions

As a set, the following questions serve three purposes. First, they focus the student's attention on a particular set of textual facts. Second, they ask students to revisit particular portions of the text that will later be considered through open-ended questions. Third, their answers provide a basis in agreement for the open-ended questions. At the same time, astute students will recognize that some of these questions may be treated as open-ended. Here, then is a set of closed-ended questions that might be used to initiate discussion:

- Who are the participants in this story?
- Why has the narrator been invited to attend the smoker?
- Whose point of view predominates in the telling of the story?
- What can we say with confidence about the setting?
- What discrete events give the story its shape?
- Whose political vision/rhetoric/stance does the narrator seek to emulate? (Additional question for research: Why/how is this important?)
- What role does the grandfather play in this story?

It is important to point out here that these questions, even though they are closed-ended, do not simply ask students to recite factual, learned information. All of these questions might invite follow up questions, depending on the need to elaborate the answers students provide. Even in tutorial settings, each student's response may add to the collective understanding being developed by the discussion participants as they work to comprehend a text or an idea by collaborating with each other.

The use of closed-ended questions might also ensure that the group's understanding of an issue or idea is in some way orthodox, that is, consistent within, say, a disciplinary focus in a field of study. The larger questions—the ideas that precede this list of closed-ended questions—will typically be these: "What must the group be aware of, and what does the group need to agree upon?" before an open-ended discussion of the text can move forward.

Open-Ended Questions

Once a common set of premises for discussion has been established through the use of closed-ended questions with a tutorial intent, the teacher is ready to move the class to a consideration of open-ended questions. We do well to remember at this point that the terms "open" and "closed" are relative, so not all answers offered in an open-ended discussion will be appropriate or correct. Again, their purpose is to bring forward interpretive possibilities. With that in mind, consider the differences between the closed-ended questions above and the open-ended questions below about Ellison's "The Battle Royal":

- What events and actions within the story seem to be symbolic? What might they symbolize?
- How does the battle royal function symbolically?
- How does the electrified rug function symbolically?
- What does the naked woman symbolize?
- What does the grandfather's deathbed message mean?
- How would you interpret the dream that the narrator relates at the end of the story?

Within the discipline of English, where the interpretation of literature is of primary interest, the most important student observations will grow from consideration of open-ended questions. While participants in an open-ended discussion necessarily share the text at hand, the possibilities for interpretation of that text multiply quickly when the burdens of exploration and examination are shared by all. This sharing of responsibility is, after all, at the heart of cooperative learning. This shared-burden approach offers a number of advantages over traditional teacher-centered discussions, and an expansive literature on constructivism supports the effectiveness of this approach.

Among the advantages of open-ended inquiry is the modeling of democratic discourse. By speaking directly to each other, students take on the burden and the opportunity to say what is true about their own cognitive landscape as well as the landscape of the text. They are free to reflect on their expectations for literary texts, on the beliefs that shape the truth as they know it, on the values that they hold, and on the ways in which truth is, in itself, negotiated within social worlds.

Conclusion

As the students' search for truth leads them toward possible destinations, it is the teacher's job to give directions, or maybe to describe the destination, but not to grab the steering wheel. Most of us remember better how we got somewhere if we had to drive ourselves. When we are chauffeured, we are less likely to remember the way. By asking open-ended questions, we allow students to provide their own transportation and take their own route. Good questions keep them going until they have reached a suitable destination—which, of course, differs with each journey. It is the teacher's charge, then, to make sure that the discussion stays focused and purposeful, though some might even argue that there is value in occasionally allowing the students to get lost.

Through a sequence of answers to a well-sequenced series of questions, an open-ended discussion becomes additive. There is greater opportunity for a classroom discussion to clarify meaning, to say what ideas a text does or does not entail, to develop those ideas, to explore complexities, to test points of view, and finally to raise subsequent questions, in Freirean fashion (82), from within the group itself. When the participants address each other, their ideas come under the scrutiny of the whole group, thus requiring that each comment gain the acceptance of the whole, not simply that of the leader.

In summary, then, closed-ended questions are useful when the primary outcomes of a discussion are enhanced knowledge and comprehension. They serve a function that is largely tutorial, and they are useful for providing orientation when the subject of discussion is difficult or unfamiliar. Discussions built around such questions are typically marked by a high degree of structure. Open-ended questions, on the other hand, enable a more comprehensive exploration of a text. They focus on both the limitations and possibilities of exploration and interpretation. Taken together, these two types of questions help us see the specific features of the textural landscape (closed-ended questions) while showing us that the vistas we describe depend on the perspective from which we view them (open-ended questions).

And finally, we might consider that the closed-ended/open-ended distinction is not really an either/or proposition. When a seemingly closed-ended question is suddenly seen to have a number of possible answers, the very premises of our inquiry are themselves called into question, and that might be the most important reason for examining questions within such categories.

Works Cited

Adler, Mortimer J., and Charles Van Doren. "The Conduct of Seminars." *The Paideia Program: An Educational Syllabus*. Ed. Mortimer J. Adler. New York: Macmillan, 1984.

Freire, Paulo. *Pedagogy of the Oppressed*. Trans. Myra Bergman Ramos. New York: Seabury, 1973.

7 Getting at What They Want to Know: Using Students' Questions to Direct Class Discussion

Mark Ensrud
Northfield High School, Northfield, Minnesota

Teachers get a fair amount of practice at generating questions. Sometimes these questions are delivered via study guides, and at other times they are fired off from the front of the classroom. Both modes for asking questions have a place in the language arts classroom. By contrast, though, the only kinds of questions my students typically ask are, "When's this study guide due?" or "Could you repeat the question?" These are hardly the kinds of questions we teachers hope for when our students are studying a piece of literature.

I am not an expert in pedagogy; I have been teaching high school English for only seven years in Northfield, Minnesota. Still, I am beginning to notice a pattern as I file my course materials away. As I go back into the file cabinets I have been organizing and filling with resources for my classes, I find that I have not used some of the resources since I first filed them. Others I have filed towards the front where I can find them easily. One I pull out often is my file on Paideia seminars, a favorite item in my teaching toolbox. My experience in using seminars lies mostly with "regular" and "advanced" ninth-grade English classes and, to a lesser degree, with seniors in college prep writing courses. While there remain some possibilities I have yet to try, I can say generally that seminars have worked well in my classes.

A Process for Teaching Student-Led Seminars

The first step for me in teaching students about seminars is to have them understand the four different types of questions: opening, closed-ended, open-ended, and core (see Figure 1). For many students, it takes some real practice before they are comfortable in writing these different types of questions, so I define the types of questions a bit more explicitly when I introduce them. Opening questions begin a discussion and invite a reexamination of the text. Closed-ended questions seek particular information, while open-ended questions invite authentic inquiry. And core questions attempt to get at the meaning of a text. Since many students have the most difficulty in writing core questions, a shorter piece such as Guy de Maupassant's "The Necklace" helps them in determining what works best.

Students first get practice in writing questions about a short story from their textbook (such as "The Necklace") that may have one theme or main idea. Our ninth-grade English curriculum is thematically based, and typically a unit will begin with a few short stories and/or poems. I have students first practice writing questions for a short story selection early in the unit. Opening questions allow students to put themselves into a character's perspective and ask questions from that viewpoint. Since opening questions are typically quite broad, students are not threatened by them. They also discover quickly that closed-ended questions are fairly easy to generate if they compare them to the multiple-choice or true/false questions they have been seeing for years on work sheets and quizzes. Once opening and closed-ended questions are quickly understood, we can focus our efforts more carefully on open-ended and core questions—the questions we hope will eventually generate the most in-depth discussion. Comparing open-ended questions to a three-year-old's persistent line of "why" questioning helps students understand these questions a bit better. Once students get a handle on open-ended questions, core questions are easier to grasp. And since the initial "practice" short story for which they are already writing questions comes under a thematic concept like "obstacles" or "relationships," it is much easier to keep students' questions related to a theme. I collect these questions and use some of them in guiding the class through a discussion of the work. It is important that students label their questions by type so that I can evaluate each question based on whether it fits the intended category. This practice allows me to check the students' understanding of the four kinds of questions before they lead a discussion using their prepared questions.

It typically takes students' reading a couple of short stories, and writing and labeling questions for them, before I am able to give ample feedback and instruction so that students are ready to move on to a whole-class seminar which I lead. Before I lead the seminar, however, I ask students to generate two questions for each category. On the day of this first seminar, I take a few minutes to explain that my role as a leader

1. Opening question. All participants can answer—serve as icebreakers, get opinions out of others. You need to have read the material to write them but not to answer them.

    a. How could prisoners of the Holocaust keep such faith in their God despite all that happened to them?

    b. What thoughts might be going through your mind if you were told that you and your family were being forced to an unknown place?

2. Closed-ended questions. There is one answer only, and the purpose is to find out what the text says: Who, what, where, when?

    a. Why did the German officers want to seize the Jews' possessions like the gold crown on Elie's tooth?

    b. How many years was it from the time Elie first came to Auschwitz to the time he was rescued?

3. Open-ended questions. Many responses are possible, and there is no single right answer. Proof is needed, and these questions are *not* written in second person.

    a. Why did the soup taste of corpses the night the little boy was hanged in the camp?

    b. What was the significance of the fork and the spoon that Elie calls "the inheritance"?

4. Core Questions. These get at the theme or main idea of the reading.

    a. How do the father-son relationships change throughout the novel?

    b. How does Elie's idea of faith change throughout the novel?

    c. Why didn't any of the Jews seek revenge when they were finally freed?

Figure 1. The four kinds of seminar questions, with sample student questions about Elie Wiesel's *Night*.

will include such things as directing discussion through the four levels of questions, asking students to refer to the text to support their answers, keeping discussion directed away from me and toward other students, and maybe offering a "starter" opening question to get things going. I also make it clear that these responsibilities will be assumed by students the next time we have a seminar. I try to follow through on my responsibilities during the class period, while also keeping track of students' participation by recording instances when they offer either a question or a valid response. After I pose a few opening questions to get people thinking and sharing ideas that may not be specific to characters or events in their reading, I will ask for four or five students to share one of their closed-ended questions. No more than ten minutes into the discussion, I will ask for someone to offer an open-ended question. After another ten minutes, in which students share their ideas on some of their classmates' open-ended questions, I will prompt someone to share a core question. We will usually discuss three or four core questions, allowing the class to identify and talk about prominent themes and ideas in the story.

After this groundwork has been laid, I give students another piece of literature and ask them to generate their own questions about it. This exercise works particularly well when we have just begun studying a novel, and I have found the progression to work best when we are beginning Elie Wiesel's *Night*. Now, instead of assigning prewritten "study guide" questions for students to answer, I sometimes have them write their own questions about this work of literature and then categorize them for the class to use in conducting a discussion of the material.

After asking students to prepare two or three questions per category about a chapter from the book, I select two students to serve in the leader role I had previously assumed, and they conduct the whole-class seminar. Once this whole-class seminar is completed, students hand in their notes on the discussion, along with questions they wrote, and I evaluate them on those items and on their participation. I usually suggest that each student try to get involved two times, either by asking a question or by giving a response, or by a combination of the two. This gives shy students something to shoot for, and those who tend to dominate discussions are encouraged to allow others the chance to speak their mind. Also, at the end of this seminar I ask students to write down feedback regarding what they liked and disliked about the seminar. Positive feedback usually includes the belief that it gave them a chance to give and exchange a variety of opinions and ideas, while negative feedback leans towards the belief that, even with the seminar format, some students still did not have a chance to participate as much as they could or might like to.

After students have gained experience with additional whole-class seminars on other chapters of the book, my next objective is to turn the leadership roles over to individual students and to set up smaller discussion groups. While I still require all students to generate questions, I will also either ask for volunteers to take on leadership roles or appoint leaders, depending on the atmosphere of the class. Before assigning students to their groups, I take some time to review the following rules:

Rules for a Seminar

1. Form a circle so people are facing one another.
2. Be *prepared*, with reading and questions completed.
3. Be courteous—there will be no put-downs and no sarcasm.

4. Allow each participant enough time to finish his or her thoughts.

5. Speak up when no one else is talking—don't raise hands unless you're desperate!

6. Be an active listener.

7. Take notes and be able to summarize a discussion.

8. Have your book open and use it for evidence.

As for group size, with my classes typically running from twenty-five to thirty students, I usually break them up into three groups while trying to avoid having groups larger than ten. I also have one student serve as recorder for the group so that I have a record of at least the sequence of questions posed during the seminar. In terms of evaluation, I assess each student's questions, assign a group score based on the recorder's notes, and give a participation score based upon observations I make during the seminars. For example, each correctly categorized question can be worth a point, the notes could be worth five points, and participation could be worth five points. The values can vary, depending upon which facet of the seminar one chooses to emphasize.

Students tend to favor small-group seminars (of ten to twelve persons or fewer) mainly because they feel more comfortable getting involved and have more chances to participate in the discussions. On the downside, some students believe that in smaller groups there is a narrower range of ideas shared. Overall, students have preferred the small-group seminar over the large-group seminar by a ratio of about two to one, so I have tended to conduct most seminars in the small-group format from that point on. (See Figure 2 for more student comments about the different types of seminars.)

As with any other way of teaching, this process results in both rewarding and frustrating moments. One of the most rewarding results is seeing the quality of questions students are capable of generating. It can be frustrating when high-quality questions are written and turned in but never posed to the group due to fear, shyness, or some other reason. It also requires some patience early on to help students develop effective questioning techniques, but this can really pay off in the long run when students take ownership of their questions and ideas.

Something else I see as rewarding in this approach is that students are in control of their learning and are capable of "finding" meaning in literature and in others' ideas. Even if students do not completely fulfill their role as seminar leaders, the rest of the group is there to push each member to find or develop answers for himself or herself because the students all know that no one else will do it for them. More important, they

84

Whole-Class Seminar

"Some people talk more than others."

"I like it because you get everyone's opinion."

"It's better than just you [teacher] asking questions."

"We need to talk more."

"It takes some getting used to because people were afraid to talk—or didn't say anything."

"Maybe we could just go around the circle and have people ask a question."

"Some people weren't listening."

Ten- to Twelve-Person Seminar

"More people got to ask their questions."

"More people got involved."

"There were still a couple people who didn't say anything."

"It didn't take as long because there weren't as many people."

"I felt more comfortable talking."

"You don't get to hear as many people's ideas and questions."

"Still some small pockets of unrelated conversation."

Small-Group (Five- to Six-Person) Seminar

"Everyone got to ask his or her questions."

"People stayed on task better."

"Everybody got involved."

"I wanted to hear more people's ideas and questions."

"Our group didn't get along so it didn't work very well."

"Our group got along real well."

"I got the chance to say everything I wanted to and ask questions."

"No irrelevant small pockets of conversation."

Figure 2. English 9 seminar feedback from students.

quickly learn that they *can* do it for themselves. (See Figure 3 for an overview of a stepwise approach to introducing this type of seminar to ninth graders.)

Some Other Possibilities I Have Tried

But what comes next? This is by no means the only way to teach and conduct seminars. I have had success with two or three different student leaders generating questions and conducting seminars in my college

Day 1

Conduct a teacher-led discussion with teacher-generated questions.

- Can be either a pre- or a postreading discussion.

Day 2

Conduct small-group student discussions with teacher-generated questions.

- Group members should play cooperative group roles.
- Ideas/responses are shared with other groups.

Day 3

Introduce the categories of questions for the seminar.

- Name categories again and have students define them and practice categorizing questions from previous two days.
- In groups of two or three, have students generate four questions (from a reading assignment), that is, one question for each of the four categories.
- It is important for students to explain/justify how each question fits its category.
- Conduct a discussion with student-generated questions.

Day 4

Introduce the concept of a seminar and provide a rationale for it.

- Provide definitions of *student-generated* and *student-led.*
- Explain the "Rules for a Seminar" list (on transparency).
- Assign reading material.
- Have each student prepare four questions—one for each of the four categories.
- Discuss evaluation of seminar.
- Circulate as students formulate questions.

Day 5

Students will take part in a seminar.

- I recommend starting with a whole-class seminar so you can model the role of leader—a role students will be responsible for in future seminars. This places focus solely on students' questions and responses (it also results in quiet spots, which can be good).
- Have students evaluate and give feedback on the process and on the seminar itself.
- Ask if the seminar was a success. Why or why not?
- Ask what students liked and disliked about the seminar.
- Ask what the students see as the benefits and disadvantages of the seminar.

Figure 3. Sample schedule for introducing the seminar to an English 9 class.

prep classes, but only in a whole-class format. I may try that approach with some ninth-grade classes. I have also experimented with even smaller groups with, say, five or six members, and I think this works best as a culminating activity with a class novel, since, given the greater opportunities to speak up in the smaller group, this arrangement usually allows the shy students to participate more fully. Another possibility is for the teacher to generate a question or series of questions before a student-led seminar and then have the student leader(s) incorporate the teacher's questions into the discussion. This approach can be effective if students are having a hard time constructing opening questions or if the teacher wants to be sure all groups discuss a certain topic or question. Thus several variations and possibilities can be employed, as long as I remember that the desired results are high-quality discussions generated and led by students.

Questions about a Seminar Approach

Questions often arise upon using the seminar approach, and two come to mind here. First, "Does each and every student get involved?" No, but many more of them do, and those who do not get involved in whole-class discussions usually get involved in small-group discussions where they feel less pressure. Second, "Do the same two or three students tend to dominate discussion?" In whole-class seminars, that is often the case, but in small groups not nearly so much. In small groups, the audience is simply not as large, and the teacher is not there to be impressed by the answer to every question. There are of course more questions about the dynamics of seminars, but many of them can be answered only by trying the seminar in the classroom.

In my classes, the seminar is not the only way to discuss literature or encourage students to get involved, nor is it the only method I use. But seminars add variety and get students actively engaged, and that is the direction I want to go. I started off with very little file cabinet space in Northfield when I first began teaching, but I am quickly learning that I will need more and more space in the very near future, particularly as I gather more resources for conducting seminars. I have not filed this information away needlessly, never to be found until another teacher comes along to clean out my files. Information on seminars is kept right near the front and accessed often.

Part II Strategies for Structuring Inquiry-Based Classrooms

8 Examining Multiple Perspectives in Literature

Elfie Israel
Pembroke Pines Charter High School, Pembroke Pines, Florida

"You mean you won't tell us the right answer?"

"There are no right answers?"

"How can her actions be both good and evil?"

"How do I take notes when so many different ideas float around and you never tell us which ones are correct?"

Questions such as these abound when I introduce Socratic seminars to my high school students. Such questions point up the fact that, all too often, students are encouraged to direct their responses to the teacher, not to their peers, and intellectual interaction among them is not encouraged.

Until this past year, I taught Advanced Placement English at Nova High School, an urban 9–12 school in Broward County, Florida. Our population was heterogeneous, drawn from all areas of the county. Almost one-fifth of our population consisted of recent immigrants.

Our students needed to pass the Florida Comprehensive Achievement Test in order to graduate, and focused seminars helped them dig deeper into the text and see a wider variety of possible interpretations. In such an approach, much depends upon the text, the teacher's preparation, and the level of trust developed in the class; but the key to this kind of inquiry is the exploration of multiple perspectives. So we were continually examining the nuances of meanings.

The Socratic seminar is a formal discussion, based on a text, in which the leader asks open-ended questions. Within the context of the discussion, students listen closely to the comments of others, think critically for themselves, and articulate their own thoughts and their responses to the thoughts of others. They learn to work cooperatively and to question intelligently and civilly.

A strong seminar text (whether a painting, poem, short story, fable, movie, or other form of text) addresses ideas and values of some complexity, often being evocative, polysemous (having many meanings), and ambiguous. Of necessity, students who examine texts of this sort will discover a variety of possible interpretations, each deriving from a different point of view.

The discourse is not a debate but a search for meaning and clarity in the text, and everyone is encouraged to participate. All opinions are valued but must be supported with evidence from the text. Asking questions and taking risks are encouraged, and it is acceptable to make a mistake, to be wrong. We ask students to embrace physicist Niels Bohr's complementarian idea that two seemingly different interpretations should be explored simultaneously.

In addition, seminars help students hone their critical thinking and creative skills. Mortimer Adler, Edward de Bono, E. Paul Torrance, and Roger Von Oech are among the educators who have devoted their research to this topic. Adler developed Junior Great Books and Great Books curricula which encourage participants to read the classics more carefully and with fuller insight. Open-ended questions by moderators encourage grappling with abstract philosophical issues. de Bono developed a curriculum which encourages students to think logically, Torrance concentrated on developing and teaching creativity, and Von Oech encouraged divergent thinking.

All of these approaches help students move from knowledge and comprehension in Bloom's Taxonomy to higher levels of cognitive processing. Students are to analyze, to apply, to create, and to synthesize. The inevitable result is a multiplicity of points of view.

The teacher's role is to prepare good, open-ended questions and then allow the students to discover what they can. Being quiet may not be easy for some teachers, but their silence is vital for conversational flow and an exchange of ideas. Teachers have a responsibility to clarify and to teach, but they may fulfill this role simply by adding factual information to the discussion.

For example, in a discussion of Jack London's *The Call of the Wild*, students in one class made no distinction between domestic pets and work animals. Realizing that this distinction was important in the story, the teacher clarified the point and then gave the discussion back to the students. Sometimes historical information must be supplied. It is difficult to teach T. S. Eliot's "The Hollow Men" or W. H. Auden's "September, 1939," without first discussing World War II, but the exploration of meaning in these texts is still up to the students.

The ideas around which many seminars revolve are often highly abstract: art, beauty, chance, courage, education, equality, experience, failure, God, happiness, immortality, law, love, nature, power, religion, sin, soul, truth, and wisdom. Both Mortimer Adler and Terry Roberts, director of the National Paideia Center at the University of North Carolina at Greensboro, have compiled useful lists (for teachers) of ideas that can serve as the focus of discussions (see Adler; Roberts and Billings). The critical factor, however, is that examination of these ideas inherently exposes multiple perspectives.

Using Texts to Demonstrate Points of View

The choice of text for classroom discussion can make all the difference for developing multiple perspectives. The possibilities, of course, are endless, but these ideas from my classroom might show the potential for encouraging various points of view.

Fathers and Sons or Existentialism?

"Musee des Beaux Arts" by W. H. Auden is an excellent text for a Socratic seminar. To provide background, one student enacted a shadow puppet show on the tale of Daedalus and Icarus. I then distributed color reproductions of the Brueghel painting "The Fall of Icarus," one for every two students.

Not informed of the painting's title, students were instructed to comment on what they saw, and they were encouraged to ask questions. It took ten minutes before a student finally commented on a small figure in the lower right hand corner that was leaning towards the water. A lively debate ensued as to whether that person was fishing or trying to help the falling Icarus. A closer examination by one student indicated that the body language did not suggest someone trying to lend a helping hand.

Much of the focus then switched to all the other figures in the painting. What was the artist saying and why were the students so oblivious to this daring experiment? They wondered why the peasants and the sailors on the passing ship seemed indifferent to the amazing sight of someone falling from the sky.

The painting became the subject of the seminar, with discussion focusing on Brueghel's possible purpose and Icarus's motives for flying so close to the sun. And, as one student asked, did the father unconsciously cause his son's death? Aren't teens known to disobey their elders? By warning him not to fly too high, did he know or think his son would rebel? The discussion turned to the issue of teenage rebellion, and the students left with varying ideas and opinions concerning the characters, the painting, and themselves.

The next day, the students read Auden's poem and discussed its meanings and implications. Do we always ignore the memorable moments in the world? Are we so materialistic, so self-absorbed, that we are unaware of others' tragedies? Are the mundane tasks of living as important as the attempts of a few to defy the gods?

A Feminist Perspective

Petronius's story "The Widow of Ephesus" seems simple on the surface, yet it led to a stimulating seminar on feminism, marital obligations, chastity, loyalty, and superstition. The questions that follow were written by my students and by me: What is your reaction to specific elements in the story, citing lines/words? What do you think of the lady? What do you think of the soldier? What lines in the text cause you to feel this way? What were some of the surprises in the story, and how did they affect you (indicate the places in the text when this occurred)? Why do you think the widow capitulates to the soldier? What do you think is the strongest bond in a relationship: love, fidelity, chastity, honor, or other, and why?

It is unlikely that any group of students will be in complete agreement as they consider these questions, and a close examination of this text can facilitate a more complex understanding of gender roles.

The Flood: Religious Story or Myth?

Because our cultural heritage includes many references to the Bible and to mythology, I tried to incorporate some of these into my lessons. Students knew that we were looking at the Bible as literature only and that God was a "character" in this book. "Noah and the Ark" was the introductory work I used for our class study of Voltaire's *Candide*. It anticipated a number of relevant questions: Why do bad things happen to good people? Why is there undeserved suffering? Is this the best of all possible worlds? How can characters' actions be both good and evil? Why are Greek stories called myths and tales from the Bible called "religious" stories?

Students listened to the segment of a Bill Moyers tape in which the story of Noah is read aloud. Then I posed this question: "Pretend you are doing a story for the front page of a paper written by Noah's children as they leave the ark. How would you describe the earth after the flood? On your papers, write only the headline for the story." To liven up the class and to reinforce the concepts of voice and audience, I give students various newspapers (the *New York Times*, the tabloid *National*

Enquirer, the *Miami Herald*,) and require that they write a headline for that particular paper. My students' responses included the following:

"Noah announces: Water shortage over. Feel free to use your sprinklers."

"What will the Lord say next?"

"Be fruitful and multiply: Part Two."

"All animals are now on the endangered species list."

"Waters receding, tempers heating."

"Divine Hostility."

"Renewal."

My students seemed to prefer this activity to summarizing the story. I also asked them, "What is the story about?" Their responses included the following: humans have faults, they are reckless and wicked, and God is omniscient yet can make mistakes. Other discussion questions included these: What kind of God is this? What did humans do to deserve this destruction? Can we say God did the wrong thing? How really wicked were the people? What does the text say and what do you think this means? Was everyone truly evil? Why are there no grays? How is this a parable, and what is it about (family, regret, lawlessness, education of God)? Is God behaving in an evil way? Can a person of faith say that God does something that is not good? (God creates good and evil.) Is this a marriage gone awry? Can we criticize God? Is this a story of retribution for lawlessness? If God is omnipotent and omniscient, how can evil exist?

Again, a wide variety of responses is invariably offered. Surprisingly, familiar stories offer the possibility of unfamiliar realizations.

Linda Pastan's "Ethics"

In anticipation of exploring this text, I showed the class an oil painting of an elderly woman and also gave each student a photocopy of one student's drawing of her grandmother. I asked them to consider the pictures of women they see in magazines, in museums, on television, and in the movies. Why were there so few of elderly women? What did this tell us about ourselves and our society's values?

I then showed them a few reproductions of Rembrandt's paintings and discussed his contribution to art. As a class, using dictionaries, we defined the word "ethics" and distinguished between it and "morals." We then read Linda Pastan's poem "Ethics" and wrote down a word or phrase in the poem that was significant to us. We went around the circle, reading the words that each student wrote down.

With a class accustomed to Socratic seminars, animated debate ensued. I then asked the students to describe their reaction to the moral dilemma posed in the poem (if a fire broke out in a museum, would they save a priceless Rembrandt painting or the life of an elderly woman?). One person was incensed that this was even a subject for discussion. Another, an artist, valued art far more than any individual life. Many students spoke about such issues as euthanasia, quality of life, suicide, and art.

We then talked about the poet's thoughts and how the students reacted to them. I asked them to pretend that they were faced with this choice and to write a newspaper headline depicting their solution. After sharing the headlines, we talked about how we deal with elderly persons in our society. I asked students how our attitudes and laws regarding elderly people were or were not ethical.

In conclusion, I asked them to share, if they would, an ethical dilemma they encountered and how they resolved it. We also discussed who or what determines society's ethics.

Steele's "Christmas Greens" and Ferlinghetti's "Christ Climbed Down"

One of my subjects was the holiday season and whether its original meanings have fallen by the wayside, so I played the song, "All I want for Christmas is my two front teeth" (Donald Yetter Gardner, 1946) and asked the students what they wanted this holiday season. (My school has students from all nationalities and backgrounds, so I tread carefully.) The responses to my question varied considerably: a new car, a computer, a trip to Italy, friendship, "a visit from my father," to get into Harvard, love.

We then read "Christmas Greens" and discussed Jenny Simper's desires and Steele's ironic bemusement. From there we moved to Ferlinghetti's poem, which is much easier to understand, though its allusions are more daunting.

What I especially liked about this lesson was that it married the didactic and the Socratic approaches seamlessly and effortlessly. I continuously took timeouts to make sure students understood the satire, the allusions, and the symbols. At the same time, the students discussed their values, what the holiday season meant to them, how it felt to be an "outsider" during this time of year, why so many suicides occur then, commercialism, and, once again, what is really important in any ethical or moral "system" and how/why this is easily forgotten.

The Awakening

Short selections work best, in part because it is easier to find textual evidence and remain focused. However, occasionally I like to put closure to a novel. One for which the seminar works well is Kate Chopin's *The Awakening*. After taking several days to discuss various parts of the work, as well as the historical, economic, and social milieu in which the book is set, I conducted our seminar. I made sure that either my opening or closing question (sometimes both) related to the students. They needed to understand the personal relevance of our discussions.

Some of the questions I posed were these: What word or words come to mind when you think of your relationship with your mom? Close your eyes and think back to when you were younger than five. If you could order a photo taken of a significant moment between you and your mom, what would you like it to be? Look at Raphael's Christ and Madonna painting. Now comment on relationship as depicted in the paintings. How does the artist make his statement?

Students then formed groups of two, and I gave each group a copy of a Mary Cassatt painting with instructions to look at it carefully and comment on the relationship between mother and child. After they offered their opinions, I followed up by asking, "What in the painting leads you to this conclusion?"

Next I asked students to think of Chopin's book and to carefully review several of the mother-child relationships. I asked them to list the relationships and then consider support from the text for any assertions/conclusions they made. I reminded them to think of actions, words, and reactions by others to the characters; and then I asked them to compare the attitudes of the mothers in the novel with what appears to be the attitude in the Cassatt painting.

This led to a variety of possible questions: What responsibilities do mothers have towards their children? How is it significant that the Pontellier children are seldom addressed by name? In what way is it meaningful (or not) that they are boys? Why would or wouldn't you like Edna Pontellier to be your mother? If you were commissioning an artist to paint a portrait of you and your mom when you were young, how would you describe the scene you'd like him or her to capture? How would you describe an ideal mother-child relationship?

The answers to these questions were predictably diverse.

Vietnam: Heroism or Cowardice?

A seminar on the Vietnam War can be based on many of the short stories written by Tim O'Brien and others, as well as on O'Brien's novel *In the Lake of the Woods.* The focus can be as diversified as the material, and possible areas of inquiry include (1) the nature of evil, (2) why bad things happen to good people, (3) why seemingly good people commit atrocities, (4) courage, (5) peer pressure, and (6) prejudice.

One of my colleagues, Peter Bayer, conducted a seminar based on O'Brien's "On the Rainy River." This story, told from a first-person perspective, recalls the narrator's receiving a draft notice and what he thought and did about it. Peter identified several "big ideas" that he wanted the students to consider: courage, obligation, duty, and honor in regard to society. The students not only read the story but also saw a video on the My Lai massacre; watched a segment of a program on the Vietnam Memorial in which the memorial's architect, Maya Lin, is maligned for her Asian heritage; and read O'Brien's short story.

The students were asked to list the values they held dear and to compare that list with the values American society holds dear. The discussion then centered on the story and its narrator: What were the narrator's internal conflicts? What conflicts did society create in the narrator? How could the students explain the last line, "I was a coward, I went to war"? In closing, students speculated about the characters they had studied in literature: What would they have done in this situation? The most interesting responses involved Huckleberry Finn and what he would do. One student was certain that Huck would flee to Canada because he wanted to escape from society. Another student countered that Huck would fight in the war because, in accordance with the ending of Twain's novel, that was the path of least resistance.

The students were then asked if they believed they had an obligation to their community or society, and if so, what it was. Most were quite solipsistic, talking about their families or themselves. Few felt any patriotism, any desire to fight for ideas or ideals. One girl, who hopes to go to West Point, did believe in a cause higher than herself, but she clearly represented a minority view.

Medea

Since Euripides' play is fairly short, a seminar works in discussing some of the main ideas: love, hate, jealousy, and revenge. I always made a list of many questions, at least two or three times as many as I expected the students to be able to discuss. Which ones I used depended upon the students' responses. I began by playing the songs "Frankie and Johnny Were Lovers" (traditional) and "Miss Otis Regrets" (Cole Porter).

A lively discussion of love and revenge ensued, a discussion which began after I asked the students to write down their definition of love. We then dealt with the play's text. In what ways was the relationship between Jason and Medea one of love? Why did it change? What did they think of the quote, "Hell hath no fury like a woman scorned"? What were their thoughts about Oscar Wilde's line, "We always kill the thing we love" in relation to *Medea*? Why did Medea kill her sons? Would she have murdered them had they been girls? One critic has said that the play is about what we fear and hate most in ourselves. Why did or didn't students agree with this view? Why did Jason marry Glauce? The students then looked at Christ's Sermon on the Mount relating to love and pondered why this advice is difficult for us to follow.

Louise Erdrich's short piece "The Shawl," which hints at infanticide, is an outstanding companion piece for this text. I also teach Toni Morrison's *Beloved,* and the question of infanticide on an even broader scale becomes quite relevant. One of my students wondered if a man's love could be "as thick" as Sethe's was for her children.

Hiroshima and the Bomb

In an attempt to develop better understanding between ourselves and others, in this case between American and Japanese people, students read John Hersey's *Hiroshima.* The culminating activity was a Socratic seminar, and, as part of their test on the book, students were asked to write three questions they might still have about the book or three questions they had expected I would ask but I did not. Then they wrote three questions that could be used in a Socratic seminar. I highlighted the better ones, typing them out and changing the wording to eliminate duplication. I added some questions of my own.

A major task was to try to find a focal point or, as Mortimer Adler would say, a central "great idea." Since the students had seen videos detailing some of the historical background, the obvious question would have been, "Should the United States have dropped the bomb?" However, desirous of avoiding a debate on a specific issue and wanting to have students talk about a more abstract idea, I chose as the focus question for the discussion "Can war ever be moral?"

I began by showing a few pictures from the Hiroshima Peace Museum and Park which revealed how the bomb had devastated the city. The students responded to the question: "Could the United States have ended the war differently?" This led to a second question: "Why bomb Nagasaki?" An animated discussion ensued. Students were shown a slide of a quote inscribed on a monument at the Peace Park in Hiroshima: "Let all souls buried here rest in peace; for we shall not repeat the evil." They discussed the "we." To whom did it refer? What does it imply? Why would some Japanese object to that pronoun? Some of the best moments were those when students asked others to either clarify their positions or to explain their statements more clearly. Those who had often spoken willingly and voluntarily deferred to others whenever possible.

The students' perspicacity was impressive. When they finally began to discuss whether or not war could ever be moral, they wondered about the objectivity and subjectivity of that question. Avoiding mention of specific wars, they discussed cultural differences and how these affect morality. They commented on ethical relativism. Darren postulated that as long as there were several aggressive individuals alive, war was inevitable. Jennifer spoke about the "testosterone factor." Nelson talked about "goodness" while Sam posited that human beings are, by nature, evil. Kawika insisted that each person had a moral code peculiar to that individual. The class then speculated about whether we, as a group, could agree upon a few moral standards.

Many times the students referred to the text for specifics about the dropping of the atomic bomb and how different the effects were from those of other wars and other bombings. Because they were familiar with Kurt Vonnegut's *Slaughterhouse Five* and O'Brien's *In the Lake of the Woods*, they cited examples from these novels to support their statements.

I was pleased that we ran out of time because I really did not want to bring closure. I hoped the topic would raise more questions than it could possibly answer. It did. I asked them, before they left the room, to think about this question: "What can we as a group and as individuals do to prevent this from ever happening again?" I was disturbed that most felt nothing could be done.

Frequently Asked Questions

Is classroom configuration important?

Yes, very much so. Chairs or desks should be arranged in a circle or a rectangle so that each person is able to see everyone else. A direct exchange of ideas among the participants is vital to the development of multiple points of view.

What kinds of texts work best for exploring multiple perspectives?

The best seminars work with texts that are closely aligned with curriculum and state guidelines. We are pressed for time in my school, between mandatory testing, field trips, block scheduling, prom and picture days, and so on. I used to meet with my students 180 hours a year. As contact time with students shrinks, it is very important to me that my seminars relate to my curriculum and to the state's standards. Otherwise, I would be unable to cover much material. In addition, this alignment gives the seminars more validity in the eyes of my scholars, and using the texts helps ground the discussions and leads to the close reading of the text which is so important both in the seminars and in the courses I teach.

Making connections is essential. For example, before assigning Margaret Atwood's *The Handmaid's Tale*, I conducted seminars on Eavan Boland's poem "It's a Woman's World," Marge Piercy's "Barbie Doll," and the Biblical passages dealing with Sarah and Hagar (Gen. 16–17, 21). Mary Cassatt's paintings can be used with books that address mother-child relationships, such as *Beloved* and *The Awakening*. A unit on transcendentalism can begin with a seminar on one of Emily Dickinson's poems. Even film clips make good texts; for instance, a seminar on heroes can use an excerpt from *Braveheart* as a text.

Comparisons among texts inevitably lead to synthesis, which promotes the development of multiple points of view.

What about the student who wishes to dominate the conversation?

Appeal to that person's better nature, perhaps by speaking to the person privately, and ask for restraint in the future. An exploration of multiple perspectives requires a variety of voices. If that doesn't work, assign that person the role of either tabulator or note taker, either at the board or at the desk. Focusing on those tasks will keep the student concentrating on the discussion, which is really the purpose of the seminar.

Must the facilitator stay out of the discussion?

No, but the purpose of the seminar is to allow for free expression of ideas with minimal interference by the teacher (though, as Socrates' dialogues indicate, the questions themselves can lead to inferences and conclusions). You may not like what you hear; however, it is best to remain silent at those moments and hope others in the class will react. Otherwise, ask a probing question concerning the response. Follow-up questions force students to reconsider their views.

In discussing Hamlet's mother, for example, one student commented that not only was marrying a brother-in-law an ancient tradition, but so was having sexual relations with stepsisters, stepbrothers, and stepfathers—since they are not related by blood. After a moment, someone in the class challenged that notion. This served as a reminder that multiple perspectives are essential in the free marketplace of ideas. If this response had not been offered, I would have posed a question to address this student's assertion.

Should students be allowed to stray from the text or bring in examples from other works?

As Holden Caulfield asserts, digression is sometimes the most interesting part. In a Socratic seminar, I try to remain focused on a main idea, but recent brain research reminds us that we learn best when we can make connections. Learning bits and pieces in isolation does not result in long-term retention. Therefore, welcome these connections, and pull students back if the discussion ranges too widely.

How might closing questions help students examine perspectives?

It is important for students to realize the relevance of the ideas discussed to themselves and their own lives. Therefore, I try to frame questions that show the relationship of the subject to the students. In discussing the morality of the atom bomb, I asked: "What can you do to prevent this evil from reoccurring?" When talking about Abraham and Isaac, I asked them to recall sacrifices demanded by parents in today's world. After conducting a seminar on Auden's "Musee des Beaux Arts," I asked the students to recount a time when they disobeyed a parent. Make the question relevant and personal to members of the class.

How is student participation evaluated?

As long as my students are on-task and listening, they receive full points for class work. Not everyone can be a leader, and some prefer to listen since they may process more slowly and privately. I usually chart at least two to three seminars a month; then I look at the charts and see if there are patterns. However, many teachers review the charts from various seminars and, after speaking to nonparticipants, may decide to reward the active ones and to reduce class participation points from the silent ones. They may also ask silent students to write reactions to comments made by three of their peers.

Postseminar writing and self-evaluations are also useful. I ask my students to synthesize, analyze, or create, based on the discussion. These assessments can take many forms, including illustrations, Venn diagrams, charts, and collages. The students can also fill out a survey about their contributions to the discussion and about what they learned.

Still, as Albert Einstein noted, "Not everything that counts can be counted, and not everything that can be counted counts." Listening, thinking, and meditating on differing ideas and interpretations are valuable and incalculable intrinsic rewards.

How does this approach fit in with the national move towards accountability?

Looking at the various ramifications of a text, reading it closely for meaning and interpretation, and then discussing it in a forum prepares students for any test. They practice critical thinking and analysis while honing basic skills. The beauty of this technique lies in the manner in which it explores the many ramifications of a particular text.

Concluding Thoughts

At first, students may feel uncomfortable with the freedom of speaking without raising hands and with no immediate gratification: "right," "correct," "wow." But in developing their thinking and speaking skills, they much prefer the respect they get from their peers to the glint in the teacher's eyes. (This is a painful lesson for us.)

They learn to peel the onion. There are no simple answers. One response or one explanation simply does not do. They also learn to listen to others and are amazed at their peers' insight.

What I personally like about Socratic seminars is their effectiveness and their philosophical underpinnings. They permit students' and teachers' minds to soar. The goals are to have civil discourse, to closely examine texts, and to think about the many ramifications of philosophical questions. I find myself questioning many of my own values and interpretations after these sessions; so do my students. They begin to accept the notion that many different ideas can float around and that none of them are necessarily correct. F. Scott Fitzgerald noted that humans can simultaneously believe in two contradictory ideas.

My students' comments at the end of the year concerning seminars are almost universally positive and enthusiastic. They do like to talk and to hear what their classmates think. I am always awed by what I have learned from them. Their perspectives, their acuity, their insights amaze me. For instance, who would have thought that when I asked them to brainstorm on the color "green" (to begin an *Othello* seminar) they would tell me that green jelly beans are an aphrodisiac?

There is no "one way only" sign for Socratic discussions. You need to experiment, to take risks. As you and your students change, so will the seminars. By liberating your mind and theirs, and by taking risks, you will ensure that you never walk into the same stream twice. I, for one, cannot think of anything more exciting and interesting.

Works Cited

Adler, Mortimer. *Six Great Ideas: Truth, Goodness, Beauty, Liberty, Equality, Justice: Ideas We Judge By, Ideas We Act On.* New York: Collier, 1984.

Auden, W. H. "Musee des Beaux Arts." *Literature: Reading Fiction, Poetry, Drama, and the Essay.* Ed. Robert DiYanni. 4th ed. Boston: McGraw, 1998. 587.

Bloom, B. S., ed. *Taxonomy of Educational Objectives: The Classification of Educational Goals. Handbook 1: Cognitive Domain.* New York: McKay, 1956.

Boland, Eavan. "It's a Woman's World." *Night Feed: Poems.* Boston: M. Boyars, 1982.

de Bono, Edward. *CoRT Thinking.* Elmsford, NY: Pergamon, 1986.

———. *Six Thinking Hats.* Boston: Little, 1999.

Erdrich, Louise. "The Shawl." *Sister Nations: Native American Women Writers on Community.* Ed. Heid E. Erdrich and Laura Tohe. St. Paul, MN: Minnesota Historical Society Press, 2002.

Euripides. *Medea.* Trans. Gilbert Murray. London: Allen & Unwin, 1975.

Ferlinghetti, Lawrence. "Christ Climbed Down." *A Coney Island of the Mind.* New York: New Directions, 1958.

Hersey, John. *Hiroshima.* New York: Vintage, 1989.

Introduction to Great Books. Chicago: Great Books Foundation, 1990.

Moyers, Bill. *Genesis: A Living Conversation.* Princeton, NJ: Public Affairs Television, Inc., and WNET New York, 1996.

O'Brien, Tim. "On the Rainy River." *The Things They Carried.* New York: Penguin, 1990.

Pastan, Linda. "Ethics." *Literature: Reading Fiction, Poetry, Drama, and the Essay.* Ed. Robert DiYanni. 4th ed. Boston: McGraw, 1998. 88–89.

Petronius. "The Widow of Ephesus." *Literature: Reading Fiction, Poetry, Drama, and the Essay.* Ed. Robert DiYanni. 4th ed. Boston: McGraw, 1998. 45–46.

Piercy, Marge. "Barbie Doll." *Circles on the Water: Selected Poems of Marge Piercy.* New York: Knopf, 1982.

Roberts, Terry, and Laura Billings. *The Paideia Classroom: Teaching for Understanding.* Larchmont, NY: Eye on Education, 1999.

Steele, Richard. "Christmas Greens." *Understanding the Essay.* Ed. Edward O. Shakespeare, Peter H. Reinke, & Elliot W. Fenander. 2nd ed. Wellesley Hills, MA: Independent School Press, 1978. 18–19.

Torrance, E. Paul. *The Search for Satori & Creativity.* Buffalo: Creative Education Foundation, 1979.

Von Oech, Roger. *A Whack on the Side of the Head: How You Can Be More Creative.* 3rd ed. New York: Warner, 1998.

9 Practicing Critical Thinking through Inquiry into Literature

John S. Schmit
Augsburg College

Some time before my second trip to Paris, I decided that I would study French by listening to a series of Berlitz CDs. Anticipating the kinds of information that I would need, I diligently practiced asking questions. Soon after I arrived, pleased with my progress and confident in my ability to make myself understood, I put my practice to the test. I was dismayed to find that, as often as not, I was completely unprepared for the stream of language that greeted my questions. In the end, I laughed quietly at my own foolishness and proceeded to accomplish what I could in English. While this brief story might seem quite unrelated to the examination of literature in a classroom setting, there is a certain similarity: answers to questions prove of little value if we are not prepared to receive them.

The understanding that we gain from our investigations into the world—whether in life, academic disciplines, or simple everyday conversation—is shaped by the questions we ask. These questions are more than simple requests for information. They entail assumptions about the kinds of information we need, what we value as information, and what we already know or believe to be true. This is the case, at least, for questions we ask on our own behalf.

What happens, though, when we ask questions of our students in a classroom discussion? Can we be sure that they share our background, our values, and our cognitive operating assumptions? There is a potential chasm between the assumptions that guide the questions we ask on our own behalf and the questions we ask on our students' behalf. We are not always certain what they know or value, and thus we can't be certain that the questions we ask them will lead them to greater understanding. It is this gap between implicit assumption and new information that produces the all-too-familiar blank stares that our discussion questions sometimes produce.

Questions for the Literature Classroom

Well-conceived inquiry into literature, then, requires more of the teacher than an ability to construct fascinating questions. It requires that students be prepared for pursuing answers to those questions. To insure this preparation, teachers must assist their students in constructing a cognitive framework to support the heft of new ideas. This scaffolding typically involves the didactic delivery of information, but it is more akin to pouring a concrete slab than framing new walls and ceilings. These latter tasks are accomplished in a series of cognitive steps, each shaped by different kinds of questions: a set of questions that, taken in sequence, will lead the student to increasingly sophisticated observations. These inquiry tasks will also make our operating assumptions explicit.

Successful class discussion requires that our questions be thoughtfully ordered. In discussions of literary texts, content issues need to be addressed before interpretive issues, so that the relevant facts of the text are clear and agreed upon before an investigation of meaning begins. This agreement comes into being when we all share the same assumptions about, for example, fruitful sources of meaning in a text, such as symbols, metaphors, or plot devices. Such questions might direct the students' attention to a set of thematic considerations, or an analysis of character construction, or an examination of the text's structure. These content questions should also anticipate later questions that will lead students to salient ideas about the text: ideas that lead them to make conclusions about the text's meaning. Then, after the discussants have come to some degree of consensus about an interpretation, a final set of questions can examine the relevance of the text to the lives of those who are interpreting it.

From the viewpoint of John Dewey, it is the last of these considerations that is most important, since students are ultimately impelled to learn by their perception of the relevance of the subject at hand (4–22). Such considerations, however, cannot be undertaken until students have first determined what a given text says and, second, have given consideration to what the text means. The careful arrangement of questions in a discussion, then, will guide the students along a cognitive path that is consistent with principles of critical thinking.

The Basic Questions

While the number of questions we might ask about literary texts is virtually infinite, they are all variations on six basic questions. These questions provide a paradigm for the construction of more specific questions about particular texts, and they are most likely to appear in the following order:

- What is _____? (knowledge)
- What is _____ about? (comprehension)
- What is _____ connected/related to? (application)
- What are the significant components of _____? (analysis)
- What does _____ mean? (synthesis)
- What is the value of _____? (evaluation)

Each of these six basic questions relates to a category of Bloom's Taxonomy of cognitive tasks, and so his list of these tasks is an invaluable resource for teachers as they construct questions (201–07).

Perhaps more important than the list itself is the order in which these tasks take place. Following Bloom's argument that such tasks are hierarchically arranged, we need to consider the cognitive progress that our students follow in the development of new ideas. There are two obvious benefits to following this scheme: (1) it ensures the best possible scaffolding of new and complex ideas, and (2) it models good critical thinking for any inquiry that these students will undertake in their respective futures.

The Phases of a Discussion

Teachers trained in the use of Mortimer Adler's Paideia model frequently hold that an ideal discussion of a text consists of three phases (Adler and Van Doren 24–29). The first phase involves exploration or discovery tasks. The second hinges on close, careful examination of ideas discovered in the first phase. The third phase extends the discussion outward from the text into the larger world. If a discussion follows this general pattern, it is more likely to move through an appropriate series of reasoning tasks. Early questions require more simple and concrete cognitive tasks, while later questions address issues that are more complex and abstract. If we relate these three phases of discussion to the questions above, we see that each phase considers two of the six basic questions.

The three phases that Adler outlined are ordered to facilitate clear understanding of the text at hand: the first, exploration or discovery, is an accounting of the contents of the text, and this is followed by an examination of the text's possible meanings, which is followed in turn by an inquiry into the relevance of the text. In the first of these steps, participants involve themselves in a discovery of facts, a recounting of experiences, or a review of observations, examples, and other pertinent information. Careful scrutiny of these building blocks of knowledge is essential to critical thinking, and so the second phase involves application and analysis of the text: What does it relate to and what are its component parts? The final step involves creating meaning and judgments as to the value and purpose of the text. Because each consideration of the text builds on the answers to previous questions, the sequencing of discussion questions is crucial.

These three phases can be used as a guide to the critical consideration of any literary text, although the purpose of each phase may differ slightly from Adler's scheme. In general, the questions that guide this first phase address the facts of the text: What is the subject of the text? When was it written? What concepts within the text seem to be important, and how can we define these concepts? Who narrates the text? How do you think the narrator feels about the subject of the text? What words or phrases seem to indicate the narrator's feelings? Once questions like these have been addressed and answered, the discussants will be prepared for a close analysis of the text.

After these discovery tasks are complete, the discussion can move on to critical considerations of the text as the students see it. While the discussion leader may assist them in deciding what questions are relevant and thus need to be asked about the text, the group still has the greatest responsibility in setting its analytical agenda. Most often, the leader will have established the purpose before the seminar, setting a context for the discussion. Once the group has agreed on the basic facts of the text, students can begin to frame relevant issues, consider pressing questions, and isolate potential answers. This is where meaning is made. Inquiry moves into interpretation and inference. In a constructivist setting, one in which students make meaning collaboratively, the group sets about the tasks of drawing inferences and refining an interpretation.

In this second phase of the inquiry process, which we might refer to as examination or analysis, important concepts are exemplified and defined, and various parts of the text are examined separately. A consideration of Robert Frost's "Mending Wall," for example, might be guided by a series of questions: What is the genre of the text? How does our knowledge of this genre shape our expectations for the text? For whom was this text originally written? How does it fit with the worldview of contemporary readers? How is it structured? Who are the characters and what are their motives? If the text is a narrative, what drives the action forward? The possibilities for questions are endless, but the concern at this stage is primarily to identify meaningful components of the text. Before constructive discussion can move forward, the group needs to be in agreement about the importance of these central concerns around which their thinking will revolve.

The final stage of the discussion addresses the creation of meaning and judgments about the degree to which the text at hand matches its potential purpose. Here, the primary questions are fairly simple: What does the text mean, and to what purpose does this meaning address itself? These questions lead students to interpretive conclusions that will need to be tailored specifically to the text at hand but that will inevitably lead students to interrogate the ways in which the text is or is not meaningful: Based on what we know about the text, what sense can we make of it? What larger contexts or intentions might lend meaning to the text? What ideas are represented or symbolized within this text? What significance or importance does the text convey? These questions about textual meaning will anticipate the students' reflection upon the text and its usefulness to their understanding of the subjects that the text brings under consideration.

Within this final stage, we might also ask students to consider contrasting points of view and to weigh any assumptions that they recognize, both those of the author and those of other members of the class. A clear examination of a text thus takes under consideration the ways in which the text presents information. Once the discussants are aware that the text has been screened through a particular lens, they may choose to focus that lens and see the text as they perceive that the author saw it, or they may impose a divergent point of view.

As inquiry moves into issues of judgment, the teacher's questions may start to depart from consideration of the text itself and move toward larger issues in the lives of the readers: How does this text ask you to reconsider your understanding of the subject at hand? How does it ask you to reinterpret the events of your own life, or issues within your own community, or ideas and values that are central to your understanding of yourself? What importance does this text hold for you?

An Illustration of the Process

Consider as an example, then, a discussion of Countee Cullen's "Yet Do I Marvel." This frequently anthologized sonnet lends itself to a variety of inquiry strategies: questions of structure, of genre, of political and social perspective, and of aesthetic quality. Students find, too, that it is a poem that repays careful, multiple readings:

Yet Do I Marvel

I doubt not God is good, well-meaning, kind,
And did He stoop to quibble could tell why
The little buried mole continues blind,
Why flesh that mirrors Him must some day die,
Make plain the reason tortured Tantalus
Is baited by the fickle fruit, declare
If merely brute caprice dooms Sisyphus
To struggle up a never-ending stair.
Inscrutable His ways are, and immune
To catechism by a mind too strewn
With petty cares to slightly understand
What awful brain compels His awful hand.
Yet do I marvel at this curious thing:
To make a poet black, and bid him sing!

The first phase, an exploration of the text, will require that students account for certain objective facts of the poem. For example, students will need to understand its mythological allusions before they can proceed to an analysis or interpretation of the text as a whole. It might also be helpful for students to understand the structure of the poem. Phase 1, then, might begin with this series of knowledge and comprehension level questions:

Phase 1 Questions

- When did Countee Cullen write "Yet Do I Marvel"? (knowledge)
- What words in this poem seem to have particular or unfamiliar meanings? (comprehension)
- Who was Tantalus? (knowledge)
- Who was Sisyphus? (knowledge)
- What do you know about the structure of this poem? (comprehension?)
- How does the content of the text give you information about the tone of the piece or about the narrator's point of view? (analysis)

The answers to these questions will mainly be factual, but objective questions such as these help the teacher emphasize that discovery results from the questions that an investigator poses. By knowing what questions are relevant to the investigation of a literary text, the reader can move toward developing a set of strategies for interpretation.

To this point, the focus of the discussion is on how the text is understood collectively, and this collective focus is crucial to critical thinking. It is literally the "common sense" of the text. This reflects our

general understanding of language. Because words themselves are symbols, all texts are, by their nature, symbolic. Thus, it is essential that the
group clarify its understanding of the text's symbol system. Each poem
is a series of representations, and so the reader has to make decisions
about what is being represented.

The discovery tasks outlined above involve the students' knowledge and comprehension of the text. These questions operate at the first
two levels of Bloom's Taxonomy. The initial stage of textual discovery
corresponds to the group's knowledge of the text. The second level,
comprehension, is accomplished as students collectively come to an
agreement about how they understand the text. To ensure a well-ordered
progression of cognitive tasks, the leader begins, then, by getting the
students to collectively investigate the text. Typically the underlying
question is "What does the text say?"

Once this common understanding has been established, the discussion moves to the next levels of Bloom's Taxonomy: application and
analysis. At this point the leader's questions direct the group to examine the text, asking in essence, "Within what possible schemes do these
ideas fit?" and, perhaps most important, "What does the text mean?"
This examination stage constitutes the core of most discussions: the time
during which meaning is constructed by the group. As the critical process moves from phase 1 to phase 2, the discussion will move from a
consideration of linguistic symbols to speculation about literary symbols. The meanings of both sets of symbols, however, will depend on
the group's interpretive decisions.

Phase 2 Questions

- Knowing that "Yet Do I Marvel" is a sonnet, where do you most
  expect to find meaning in it? (application)
- What connections do you see between the structure of the poem
  and its content? (application)
- What images or references in the text function symbolically?
  (application)
- What might the blind mole represent? (analysis)
- Why does the narrator mention Tantalus and Sisyphus? (analysis)
- What do you think the poem means? (analysis)
- Bearing this meaning in mind, how do you think the plight of a
  black poet resembles the fates of the mythological characters
  named within its text? (synthesis)

The first three of these questions focus on what Bloom would call the
task of application; they ask where the ideas discovered by the group

might fit within a larger scheme. When readers of the text have answered these questions, they should have arrived at a satisfactory interpretation.

Typically, as the search for meaning comes to a close, participants in the discussion will begin to shift their attention to issues beyond the text. In some cases, this is an appropriate place for the leader to bring the discussion to a close. In other cases, though, the leader may direct the group to examine the relevance of the text at hand—to discover applications for the text by focusing on analysis, synthesis, and evaluation questions:

Phase 3 Questions

- In what ways does Cullen's poem create perspectives that agree or disagree with others that you have examined in your reading of literature? (analysis)

- In what ways does the poem create perspectives that reflect your own understanding of the world in which you live? (synthesis)

- In what ways, if any, has this poem broadened your understanding of the world in which you live? (synthesis)

- How does this text relate to your own life? (synthesis)

- Why is this text important? Or why isn't it important? (evaluation)

The first question requires an analysis of narrative perspective; it asks readers to identify patterns of perception that are either consistent or inconsistent with their own. The second and third questions lead the group to synthesize: to compare newly discovered ideas from the text at hand with ideas conceived in earlier discussions or from prior experiences. The final question is evaluative, asking students to weigh the value of the text, as well as the value of their new ideas.

To review the process then, the leader's open-ended questions focus on knowledge and comprehension. The central questions that occur toward the middle of the discussion draw out the meaning of the text through application and analysis. Lastly, should the leader deem it appropriate to the group, a final set of questions may lead the group to find extensions of the meaning discovered through synthesis or evaluation.

Some Conclusions

The construction and ordering of questions is an important consideration for inquiry learning. By giving thoughtful attention to the needs of students and to principles of critical thinking, teachers can ensure that the direction of the discussion is rigorous and productive. Careful ordering of questions will help students build understanding effectively by assuring that each required task within the inquiry process is properly scaffolded.

Works Cited

Adler, Mortimer J., and Charles Van Doren. "The Conduct of Seminars." *The Paideia Program: An Educational Syllabus*. Ed. Mortimer J. Adler. New York: Collier, 1984. 15–31.

Bloom, Benjamin S. *Taxonomy of Educational Objectives: The Classification of Educational Goals. Handbook 1: Cognitive Domain*. New York: McKay, 1956.

Cullen, Countee. "Yet Do I Marvel." *On These I Stand: An Anthology of the Best Poems of Countee Cullen*. New York: Harper, 1947. 3.

Dewey, John. *The Child and the Curriculum, and The School and Society*. Chicago: U of Chicago P, 1956.

10 Moral Development and Meaning in Literature: A New Approach to Inquiry

Martha Strom Cosgrove
Edina High School, Edina, Minnesota

In 1999 at Henry Sibley High School in Mendota Heights, Minnesota, as our English department planned a new course, we began with our own inquiry: how can we design a multicultural literature-based course without constructing a "drive-by" curriculum? We didn't want to develop a course reminiscent of the old movie *If It's Tuesday, This Must Be Belgium*. Though we faced some obstacles—for example, the teachers didn't have a deep knowledge of world literature to draw on, and our students would come to us with very little background—we were motivated by our desire to talk to students about ideas that we thought mattered, to them and to us. We wanted a better reason to read the Greeks than the usual: "They've always been taught, always been considered important," or, worse yet, "It's high culture; it's good for you." We knew that *we* read Greek literature because it was meaningful to *us*. Couldn't it be meaningful to students, too, and if so, how could we make it meaningful?

Our answer came from an unlikely consideration. We had been disturbed by our belief that not many adults talk to high school students about ethics. Our conversations about academic honesty, for example, fell on curious ears. We wondered if we could construct a curriculum to help our students develop into thoughtful human beings rather than random consumers of cultural products. Should we even get into such a thicket? As we pondered these questions, we found ourselves reflecting on Lawrence Kohlberg's theory of moral development.

Kohlberg's theory might not be everyone's immediate answer to our dilemma, but it was ours. Drawing from a brief article by Kohlberg and Richard H. Hersh on the six moral stages, we realized that this developmental theory could provide us with a course framework that was broader and sturdier than those used in many high school English class-rooms. Most of our courses presented students with genre-based or chronological survey courses. Neither of these frameworks had done much to help us sell the profound meaning of literature that we found in our own lives. So, we looked at how we might make use of Kohlberg's developmental theory.

Examining Kohlberg's Theory

Our curricular inquiry began, then, with an examination of Kohlberg and Hersh's text. We felt we were really onto something when we read the following short paragraph:

> Moral development . . . does not simply represent an increasing knowledge of cultural values. . . . Rather, it represents the trans-formations that occur in a person's form or structure of thought. The content of values varies from culture to culture, hence the study of cultural values cannot tell us how a person interacts with his/her social environment, or how a person goes about solving problems related to his/her social world. This requires the analysis of developing structures of moral judgment which are found to be universal in a developmental sequence across cultures. (p. 54)

We were also interested in the relationship between moral development and cultural values, and in the relationship between the abstract think-ing needed for moral thinking and what we in education call critical thinking. After all, how could students even begin to approach litera-ture without the ability to think abstractly? It seemed that abstraction was at the core of everything.

Our goals for our new course were three-fold. First, we wanted to support the critical thinking skills lauded by Bloom (201–7) and Marzano (19–21). Second, we wanted students to encounter literature from a wide variety of eras and places. Finally, we wanted our students to be actively engaged in the construction of their own learning, and, in fact, in the construction of themselves. We named the new course "Studies in Literature: International Voices."

Before we could start matching works of literature with moral stages, though, we had to make the moral stages accessible to high school juniors. So we created an overhead transparency to help us talk to students about moral reasoning.

Investigating Stages of Moral Reasoning in Literature

Introducing Kohlberg's Theory of Moral Development was the key to this course. Though the literature was most important (and we discussed

far more than questions such as "What stage do you think this character is on?"), Kohlberg's model was what connected everything. It was
what made the course a coherent whole rather than a series of interesting and important works. To bring students along, we needed to be clear,
convincing, and quick; so we introduced the model in one class period.

First we talked about how children develop. Most students have
experiences with children and know that babies first roll over, get on
their knees, rock back and forth, and then crawl. We recalled toddlers
"cruising" around furniture, letting go, and taking first steps to the
cheers of parents. We mentioned Piaget as a figure who has articulated
developmental stages (Piaget and Inhelder 122–27). Then we linked to
the suggestion that there are stages of moral and ethical development,
too. Lawrence Kohlberg is one who theorizes about such stages. I usually mentioned that his is not the only framework; there is Carol Gilligan,
too, whose ideas we considered later in the year (3–19).

Then, with a transparency titled "Stages of Moral Reasoning" and
distilled from the Kohlberg and Hersh article, we discussed the six stages
with students (see Figure 1). I was most inclined to have students create their own notes, but if the group needed more support I might give
them a handout with the explanation of each level and let them fill in
the information about the stages and examples. With stages 1 and 2, we
talked about toddlers wanting another child's toy and just taking it. I
might see a student with a cool pen or book and, while I was talking,
just walk over and take it to provide us with a classroom-based example.
If the student didn't object, I'd suggest this was stage 1 behavior on my
part. If the student objected and I had to return the object and be sneaky
about getting something else from another student, I'd be demonstrat-
ing stage 2 behavior: serving my own interests (wanting the object) but
anticipating another's reactions (objecting to my taking the object) by
being sneaky about getting it.

The conversation usually bounced back and forth from preschool
examples to my in-class examples. Preschool examples for stage 3 and
stage 4 recalled the lesson from parents, "If you want a friend to play
with, you'll have to share." In other words, you'll have to suppress your
desires and impulses for the larger fun of playing with a group. In classroom terms, you have to take turns and be respectful in discussion to
get the larger gain of learning with a group, hearing others' ideas.

About this time, someone would observe that he knew an adult
stuck in stage 1 or 2. Moral and ethical development is not achieved simply by age. Students love this. They see pretty quickly that it is possible
for them to be further along in their development than the adults in their
lives. But usually students want to leave the stage 1 and 2 behaviors

---

Stages of Moral Reasoning

First Level

In the first level, people operate as individuals rather than as members of a group or social system.

Stage 1—People focus on their own interests and have little or no sense of responsibility to others. "Right" is what is not punished.

Stage 2—People want to serve their own interests but are able to anticipate another's reactions. "Right" is what satisfies one's own needs.

Second Level

In the second level, people begin to see themselves as members of a group or society. The social order has value.

Stage 3—People can see the value of caring, trust, and respect between individuals. "Right" is what gains the approval of others.

Stage 4—People begin to reason as members of a social system. "Right" is obeying authority in order to maintain the social order.

Third Level

In the third level, people attempt to define moral principles that have validity in and of themselves, regardless of the group to which an individual belongs.

Stage 5—People recognize that individual rights have been generally agreed upon by society. "Right" is respecting the rights of others and supporting the principles upon which society is based.

Stage 6—People make moral decisions based on self-chosen ethical principles that satisfy criteria such as logic, universality, consistency, human rights, respect for others. "Right" is what is ethical and supports human worth and individuality.

Figure 1

behind. I once had a student absolutely quit eating pretzels during class the day after the introductory lesson because she didn't want to see herself as a stage 2 person.

In the discussion of stage 5, we would talk about principles (perhaps not moral ones) on which a classroom is based: being on time, taking turns in discussion, being respectful of others' ideas. These are the principles the classroom society agrees on. Then we would shift to the national perspective, and students would typically suggest that the moral principles of our society are tolerance and the freedom to express individuality.

We can make the lofty and abstract nature of stage 6 concrete with one name: Martin Luther King Jr. Most students "get it" instantly, but we would break it down so all students understood that the principle one stands up for in stage 6 is a moral one that shall be universally applied. On the contrary, speeding just because driving 55 feels too slow is *not* stage 6 behavior. This contrast was all it took. I would have students bring a "real life" example of each of the six stages to class the next day for us to sort through to check for misunderstanding, and with this we were ready to go.

Applying Kohlberg's Theory to Selected Readings

To ensure students' understanding of the developmental framework, we found ourselves asking them to consider some big questions. As we looked at the first level we wondered, What do individuals want? This is the stage ascribed to early childhood through later adolescence, so we asked students to remember their own childhood or to think about their own younger siblings. What are the interests of the individual, when considering the individual only? What does this mean from the perspective of the child? I want—food, toys, things. Students thought that at this level it is important that the child's need be satisfied *right now!* They also thought individuals want affection, security, a connection to other human beings. When students expressed their knowledge of adults who behave this way or who are "stuck at the level typical of toddlers and preteens," they usually concluded that this was a pitiful state of affairs, and they began to see the value of "moving up."

The readings we selected for this unit dealt with primary human desires, such as the basics of food, clothing, shelter—but also the desire for love, companionship, self-respect. The characters in these works were motivated by their primary self-interest. In "The Glass of Milk" we see a man lacking the very basics needed for survival but also needing love and self-respect. In "The Pearls," the literal need seems to be for love; but when we look more carefully, control emerges. Students then consider whether control is a "primary" need. Altogether, we included the following works from our anthology text, *World Masterpieces* (Corcoran et al.), in this first unit:

"The Glass of Milk," Manuel Rojas

"Significant Moments in the Life of My Mother," Margaret Atwood

poetry by Sappho and Catullus

excerpts from *The Rubaiyat of Omar Khayyam*

"The Pearls," Isak Dinesen

"The Overcoat," Nikolai Gogol

The Deserted Crone, Zeami

excerpts from *Tao Te Ching*, Lao Tzu

"Substance, Shadow, Spirit," T'ao Ch'ien

poetry by Tu Fu and Li Po

We looked at the main character in each text and tried to discern which level or stage that character was *fundamentally* operating on. Where the character might be "placed" and why was never the only thing we discussed in class, but those discussions were always lively. The discussion often aroused questions about the extent to which a character was operating within a particular stage. Such consideration elicits student understanding of the complexity of characters, and of human beings.

One story we read, "The Glass of Milk," tells of a proud sailor who so loves the sea that he will take any job, however meager the pay, to be ocean bound. We meet him when he takes a one-week job, with pay due at the end of the job. He has no resources from previous work. He asks the foreman for an advance, but his request is denied and he makes no effort to plead his case. He is too proud to show how vulnerable he is and refuses to take any charity from other workers. Nearly collapsing from hunger, he goes into a cafe and orders milk and cookies from a maternal waitress who can see his desperate situation. She says nothing, but she is kindly, and he receives the food, breaking down in tears. He leaves without paying, goes to the beach, and sleeps on the sand with his face toward the sea.

This story centers on what the individual wants and needs. It presents a complex assortment of desires, including the basic need for food, but also the need for caring, understanding, love. We can also talk about the need for work, and for work that is meaningful. How one "goes after" what one wants and needs reveals the stage the character seems to be in. He needs food and finally goes into the cafe and orders food he knows he cannot pay for. He is violating the agreed-upon custom, and this is not stage 6 behavior. This seems to be stage 1 behavior—he is taking what he desires, but do the circumstances (being near starvation) change how we judge his action? He wants and needs work that is meaningful and goes after it, but to such an extreme degree (he won't take a job that is not on the sea) that he nearly perishes. Like a toddler who wants the other child's truck, he wants to work on the sea, regardless of the consequence. Another fundamental desire of human beings is revealed by his extreme reaction to the kindness of the waitress: the need for another human being to understand and care for us.

We placed this story with Level 1: "People operate as individuals rather than as members of a group or social system." We can see the character's need for food, clothing, shelter, but also his need for love and for meaningful work.

Then we moved to the second level, where "people begin to see themselves as members of a group or society." Here a person sees that social order has value, so our class discussion explored what happens when people begin to see themselves as members of a group or society. As children, when does this happen? When we meet at the sandbox or join a playgroup? What does the individual have to give up to be part of a group? In the sandbox I can't simply take your truck, because if I do then I won't have playmates next week. But what happens in a middle school? Students can readily remember how much of their true selves they gave up to be accepted by a desired group. How does that work in the larger adult world, do you suppose?

In order to answer this question about the reshaping of individual identity, our unit question became "What does society want?" Students predictably concluded that society wants "to stay the same." The status quo is desirable because it reflects the means by which society endures. Pericles tries to sell us on the nobility of surrendering a human life so that Athens will endure—well, maybe Athens is worth the sacrifice of human life, but what about Vietnam, or Bosnia? We included the following works in this unit:

"Pericles' Funeral Oration," Thucydides

"A Call to Arms," Callinus

excerpts from *The Prince*, Niccolo Machiavelli

excerpts from *The Analects,* Confucius

Kohlberg's second level, then, reflects the rules agreed upon by the members of the social system. Students understand that individuals give up some autonomy for the advantages of becoming part of a social system.

It became clear early on that the desires of the individual and the desires of society often come in conflict. We departed from Kohlberg for a bit to answer the question burning in the mind of all adolescents: "What if I don't obey?" How do those conflicts between individuals and society get resolved? We discussed laws, the freedoms they sometimes require us to give up, and the benefits they provide for the individual. "My Melancholy Face" and "The Metamorphosis" both present an arbitrary social system with which we see characters earnestly trying to comply. Students are outraged that the individual is sacrificed. Oedipus presents a more complex problem because of his dual role as a leader and a private individual. The works we considered in this unit follow:

Oedipus the King, Sophocles

"My Melancholy Face," Heinrich Boll

The Metamorphosis, Franz Kafka

"The Myth of Sisyphus," Albert Camus

Can there be a resolution? War and death offer options, but high school students quickly recognize that neither of these is really a genuine resolution. Literary works such as *A Doll's House* suggest a metaphorical death—not much of an improvement. We now embed the discussion of Kohlberg's third level, when people attempt to define moral principles that have validity in and of themselves, regardless of the group to which an individual belongs: Do characters operate from universal principles that support human worth and individuality? In fact, hardly ever. We examined the following works:

excerpt from Plato's *The Apology*

A Doll's House, Henrik Ibsen

excerpt from Dante's *Inferno*

excerpt from Johann Wolfgang von Goethe's *Faust*

In struggling to find a "hopeful" resolution to the conflict between the individual and society, we realized that this is one thing art does. Art can be the resolution. Art can do other things as well, but in the works we included in this unit we explored the purpose of art for the individual, the audience, and society. In discussing the motivation of the artist, we see both commercial motivation in "The Infant Prodigy" and the creator who desires only personal expression in "The Artist." What meaning does art have for the creator? The audience? What is the "correct" meaning—what the artist intends or what the audience understands, or a combination of both? It is in this discussion that students come to understand that with literature, as with visual art and music, they can make an essential contribution to the meaning of the work. Works we used in the discussion included the following:

The Tempest, William Shakespeare

"One Great Heart," Alexander Solzhenitsyn

"The Artist," Rabindranath Tagore

"The Infant Prodigy," Thomas Mann

Naturally, we had many conversations about literature that focus on conventional topics such as plot, theme, character development, conflict resolution, style, figurative language, and so on. These elements continued to occupy a very important place in our classes. However, our discussions of themes and characters' motivations became colored by Kohlberg's framework. As it turns out, the connection between literature and life, the question of students' ability to link themselves and their world to the literature, seemed to be infused with more genuine meaning. Students were surprised to discover that they are the creators of meaning.

Getting Results

When students wrote during the following year about books that had changed their lives, they often mentioned works we read in our "Studies in Literature: International Voices" course. For instance, Evan commented on how Oedipus both affirmed his knowledge and shifted his perspective, priorities, and life goals: "Books have changed my life by showing me that I shouldn't take everything seriously. For a while I was a pretty serious guy. I wanted to get rich and I really didn't care about much else. Reading books like *Oedipus* showed what I already know, one day I was going to die. I always knew it, but books like *Oedipus* that showed that fate was inescapable made me be conscious of it. This is a major turning point. Trivial things like money aren't important when you realize how short life is."

Maggie, having read Jane Goodall's *A Reason for Hope*, integrated her own interest in the natural world and her optimism with two works from nineteenth-century Russia and twentieth-century South America: "Since Jane Goodall talked all about hope in her life and how important it is and where she finds it, I was thinking about our first paper last year. I wrote it on 'The Overcoat' and 'The Glass of Milk.' These stories also have a lot to do with hope. I guess now more than ever in my life I understand the importance of hope in living a life. Both of these stories demonstrate this."

When I moved to another district this past fall, I left this course behind. As I plan the American Literature course I am currently teaching, I can't help but think about discussing *The Great Gatsby* in terms of Kohlberg's first level. I think about whether Willy Loman in *Death of a Salesman* is an individual surrendering to the conflict between the individual and society. Are the troubles in Tim O'Brien's *The Things They Carried* to some extent due to the lack of consensus between the people and the government about the individual rights supposedly agreed upon by society? This framework, focusing as it does on Kohlberg's model, allows teachers and students to talk about literary matters, and matters of life. It makes both more important.

Works Cited

Bloom, Benjamin S. *Taxonomy of Educational Objectives: The Classification of Educational Goals. Handbook 1: Cognitive Domain.* New York: McKay, 1956.

Corcoran, James, et al., eds. *World Masterpieces.* Englewood Cliffs, NJ: Prentice, 1991.

Gilligan, Carol. "Adolescent Development Reconsidered." *Mapping the Moral Domain: A Contribution of Women's Thinking to Psychological Theory and Education.* Ed. Carol Gilligan, Janine Victoria Ward, and Jill McLean Taylor. Cambridge, MA: Harvard UP, 1988. 3–19.

Kohlberg, Lawrence, and Richard H. Hersh. "Moral Development: A Review of the Theory." *Theory into Practice* 16.2 (1977): 53–59.

Marzano, Robert J. *Dimensions of Thinking: A Framework for Curriculum and Instruction.* Alexandria, VA: Association for Supervision and Curriculum Development, 1988.

Piaget, Jean, and Bärbel Inhelder. *The Psychology of the Child.* Trans. Helen Weaver. New York: Basic, 1969.

11 Critical Inquiry Strategies for Responding to Social Worlds Portrayed in Literature

Richard Beach
University of Minnesota

In responding to literature, students are actively engaged in constructing social worlds. As they enter into and roam around in these imagined worlds—looking at goals, roles, rules, beliefs, and traditions that shape the characters' practices—they are attempting to understand each character's behavior within the larger context of these social worlds.

This conception of social worlds goes beyond somewhat limited notions of the term "setting," which is often used to indicate a geographic location or social place. Social *worlds,* in contrast, entail larger cultural and psychological forces constituting the meaning of practices within that world. Thus, the social world of a Puritan community in *The Scarlet Letter* is more than simply a village populated by Puritans. It is a world of practices, activities, and beliefs constituted by the Puritan religion which defines what it means, for example, to engage in "sinful acts."

And this conception of social worlds focuses on characters not as individual entities perceived as outside of society but as entities operating within a social world. For example, in a familiar unit such as "The Individual versus Society," characters such as Holden Caulfield are valorized for not conforming to the dictates of "society," as if these characters could exist in a realm that transcends society.

Studying Social Worlds in Literature as Activity Systems

One way of thinking about these worlds is to consider them as "systems." We are all familiar with the concept of "learning the system" as it is applied to learning the ropes in a new school, institution, or workplace. David Russell defines an activity system as "any ongoing, object-directed, historically conditioned, dialectically structured, tool-mediated human interaction. Some examples are a family, a religious organization, a school, a discipline, a research laboratory, and a profession" (510). Activity systems are driven by large motives or objects, and participants learn to use certain practices, tools, rules, and roles designed to achieve their motive or object. For example, in the activity system of a political campaign, candidates and campaign workers are engaged in achieving an object—winning an election. To achieve that object, they employ various tools—press releases, campaign ads, polls, door-to-door visits, and so on. They also adhere to certain rules or conventions associated with running a campaign (e.g., funding limits and ethical norms) and adopt various roles (e.g., manager, communications director, fund-raiser, or speechwriter).

Activity systems such as schools, families, companies, clubs, organizations, sports teams, or communities are never static; they are continually evolving as the status quo becomes inadequate—that is, as students are not learning, family members are not getting along, or the company is losing money. These actions might therefore precipitate the need for new ways of operating.

Interpreting social worlds in literature as systems encourages students to adopt a critical stance related to the limitations of a system. Carole Edelsky posits that "being critical means *studying systems*—how they work and to what end—focusing on systems of influence, systems of culture, systems of gender relations. . . . [B]eing critical means questioning against the frame of a system, seeing individuals as always within systems, as perpetuating or resisting systems. Being *non*critical . . . means seeing individuals as outside of . . . [and] separate from systems and therefore separate from culture and history" (28).

Thus, attending to systems moves one away from the highly individualistic focus of much of current literature instruction. As is evident in units such as "The Individual versus Society," students are often taught to perceive characters as individual "real people" assumed to be "outside" of or at odds with society (Mellor and Patterson). Interpreting characters as operating within social worlds as systems helps students recognize how characters are shaped by those systems.

In focusing on social worlds in literature as systems, students are critically analyzing the tensions between the status quo and the need for systems to change or improve. As Jerome Bruner argues, literary narratives revolve around conflicts between, on one hand, hopes, desires, and dreams of potential new systems and, on the other hand, the reality of existing systems geared to the status quo. In *Of Mice and Men*, for example, Lenny dreams of owning his own farm, a dream that conflicts with the reality of a migrant farm system that exploits migrant workers. In *Huckleberry Finn,* the existing system works to preserve a racist, segregated status quo. Huck initially operates in such a status quo system—a traditional middle-class, segregated, small town (Engeström). During his adventures on the river, Huck challenges this system through his anarchistic "lighting out" on the river with Jim. Huck is trying to create a new system, an integrated society that moves beyond the conventional, bourgeois life of his town. For Engeström, Huck is caught between membership in his small town's attempt to maintain the segregated status quo and his allegiance to a new, emerging system that challenges this status quo.

Faced with these challenges to and breakdowns in the system, forces of the status quo attempt to preserve or protect a system that benefits them by squelching or blocking changes. Characters who challenge the status quo must carefully plan their actions in order to achieve the object of maintaining or changing the system.

These "systems" are not located "in" texts. Students construct these systems by drawing on related lived-world experiences in peer-group, school, familial, community, and workplace worlds. Some find that these worlds are congruent with each other—that they can readily transfer practices valued in one world to another; for example, for some, the middle-class practices of their home may also be valued in their school (Phelan, Davidson, and Yu). Others find that social worlds are incongruent or incompatible; for example, their school devalues or excludes their cultural background and practices—for example, the fact that Spanish is their primary language. They experience a range of borders between these incongruent social worlds, in some cases perceiving them as overwhelming but in other cases perceiving them as negotiable. For example, students may experience such a wide gap between their home and school culture that they give up on school. Students who have difficulty negotiating these borders report that they are rarely given much guidance or instruction on how to do so (Phelan, Davidson, and Yu). In responding to literature, students can draw on these experiences of negotiating borders and barriers between different worlds to interpret characters' experiences in competing worlds as systems.

A Model of Critical Inquiry for Constructing Social Worlds

In this chapter I put forth a model of inquiry involving a set of critical strategies to be used in constructing various components of social worlds as systems (for a complete description of this model, see Beach

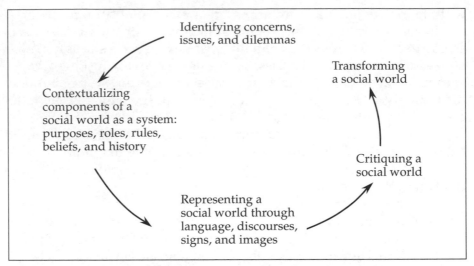

Figure 1. Critical inquiry strategies for constructing social worlds.

and Myers). I will then illustrate the application of this model with middle school and high school students.

Critical inquiry involves having students learn to interrogate the limitations of social practices operating in a system (Short and Harste; Wells). This critical inquiry model revolves around a series of recursive strategies involved in analyzing systems as constructed through language, discourses, signs, and images (see Figure 1).

Students initially immerse themselves in a text in order to identify a concern, issue, or dilemma that resonates with them in terms of their real-world experiences. For example, in responding to Barbara Kingsolver's novel *The Bean Trees*, students may express their concern about the fact that the system provides little or no support for the main character, Taylor, as a single mother. Having identified this concern, students might then contextualize or frame it within the larger context of a social world. They might, for example, consider how various components of a social world as a system—its objects/motives, roles, rules, beliefs, and history—constitute the meaning of practices within that world. They might also examine how characters in these worlds represent their experiences through means including language, narratives, signs, genres, and artifacts. All this may then lead to students' critiquing the components operating in a system—for instance, the repressive rules shaping practices in a system. This critique may in turn lead to transforming—entertaining some alternative ways to revise or change a world for the better.

I will discuss each of these inquiry strategies as employed by teachers in two different inquiry projects at different grade levels. The first involved a group of fifteen seventh-grade females who volunteered to meet in an after-school group (called the Girls' Book Club) organized by Sarah Gohman, a middle school teacher at Wayzata Middle School, Wayzata, Minnesota. The focus of their inquiry project was the social world of the Middle Ages as portrayed in the Newbery Honor Book *Catherine, Called Birdy* (Cushman). The novel, written in diary form, portrays the life of an adolescent female, Catherine, whose father wants to marry her off to an older suitor whom she despises.

The second project was conducted in Kim Van Voorhees's eleventh- and twelfth-grade literature class at Osseo Senior High, Osseo, Minnesota. In this project, students studied the world of the American West as portrayed in the novel *Montana, 1948* by Larry Watson. Set in a small Montana town in 1948, the novel portrays the conflicts within a family as told by a twelve-year-old boy, Davy. The main character, the town's sheriff and the boy's father, faces the dilemma of having to put his own ne'er-do-well brother in jail for the rape of an American Indian woman. The sheriff's and brother's father tries to protect the brother, creating a tension between the sheriff and his father.

Identifying Concerns, Issues, and Dilemmas

As they respond to texts, students tend to identify concerns, issues, or dilemmas portrayed in texts or derived from students' own experiences. They are bothered or disturbed by these considerations to the point of wanting to know more about them. With this in mind, the Girls' Book Club group, working in pairs, first studied specific aspects of medieval life, such as the feudal system, the life of lords and peasants, the church, and education. Each pair shared what they had learned with other group members and then read and shared their responses to *Catherine, Called Birdy*.

In their dialogue journals, the girls responded to prompts such as "How do you feel about the way Catherine is treated by her father?" and "Would you enjoy living in this society?" Many of the students were concerned about Catherine's treatment as a female by her authoritarian father—specifically, his attempt to marry her off against her wishes. They noted the constraints on her as a female, as well as the lack of opportunities to receive an education or choose to work outside of the home. Through voicing these concerns about women's status, students then had some basis for exploring this topic further.

They also identified issues that would serve as the basis for their inquiry projects. Framing inquiry projects around issues focuses attention on competing perspectives and agendas that are operating in a system. The girls discussed the issue of whether men were more likely to succeed in fighting in the Crusades because they were perceived as stronger than women. They discussed the fact that some women did fight in the Crusades and how this might have led to change for women in general. They were particularly perplexed by the power that religion played in politics and were baffled that people were physically punished for not believing in Roman Catholicism. They wondered how people would learn to truly understand the teachings of the Bible if they weren't allowed to question its meaning. Framing their responses in terms of issues meant that they then wanted to explore larger social and political forces shaping characters' lives. They also wanted to connect issues relevant to the medieval period to current issues such as the roles of the church and of religion, of gender status, and of education in their own lives.

Kim's students began their inquiry about the American West by listing associations with the concept "the American West." Students listed items such as cowboys, American Indians, ten-gallon hats, saloons, guns, horses, "the frontier," ghost towns, tumbleweeds, ranches, sheriff, dirt, wind, dreams coming true, glitter and gold, Hollywood, movie stars, and the allure of California. The class then discussed differences between these items and the contemporary West, noting disparities between the Hollywood version of the contemporary, post–World War II West and a more realistic version of the West characterized by declining small towns, sprawling urban areas, ethnic strife, uneven agricultural economies, and environmental degradation.

The students then discussed their reactions to the novel *Montana, 1948*, comparing the portrayal of the small town and the conflicted family in the novel with the Hollywood versions of the west. Students noted that while Davy expects that his father as sheriff should be carrying a gun and wearing a badge and cowboy hat or boots, he actually has a law degree, wears a shirt and tie, and seems to lock up only the town drunk. Working in small groups, the students then discussed issues associated with related disparities between myths and realities. One group talked about the difference between the myth of the "happy family" portrayed in 1950s television programs and the realities of family conflict portrayed in the novel. Another group discussed the stereotyped portrayal of American Indians in Hollywood movies as contrasted with the complex American Indian characters in the novel. Another group noted the "eye-for-an-eye" justice system operating in Hollywood Westerns, which conflicts with the legal system adhered to by Davy's father. And another group examined the marginalization of women in the Western as contrasted with the portrayal of women in the novel. In their discussions, students cited quotes from the novel that served to verify their identification of these disparities between myth and reality.

Students might also build their inquiries around characters' dilemmas (or their own) for which they have no easy answers or solutions. Peter Mosenthal notes that dilemmas are defined by competing social agendas: "do drugs now and be part of the peer group with the risk of being caught; don't do drugs, avoid the risk of being caught, but be scorned by peers" (340). He cites the example of *Romeo and Juliet,* in which the young lovers are caught between two conflicting goals—having to please their warring families and wanting to marry against their families' wishes. The Girls' Book Club group perceived Catherine in *Catherine, Called Birdy* as caught in a dilemma from which she has no escape. She wants to experience love, but not in the form of a forced marriage to someone she despises. By rejecting her father's attempt to marry her off, she also faces being ostracized by him. Identifying Catherine's dilemma led students to examine the competing social agendas of her need to survive economically versus her need for autonomy.

Kim's students noted that Davy's father is caught in the dilemma of having to bring his own brother to justice for crimes against an American Indian woman, efforts that are opposed by Davy's grandfather and some townspeople.

Contextualizing Social Worlds in Literature

Having identified certain concerns, issues, or dilemmas, students then contextualize them within the framework of the social worlds portrayed in literature. They attempt to explain these concerns, issues, or dilemmas in terms of various forces operating in a social world, such as purposes, roles, rules, beliefs, and history (Beach and Myers). For example, having identified a major concern as Catherine's conflict with her father, Sarah's students examined how that conflict stemmed from the family's sense of *purpose*, the *roles* family members assign to each other, the *rules* governing decision making in the family, or *beliefs* about power and privilege in the family. In all of this, they were focusing on more than just individual characters; they were examining how these components of social worlds shaped characters' actions.

In studying the purposes or objects driving such systems, students might ask, "Why are people doing what they are doing? What are they trying to accomplish? What is driving their participation in an activity? Are there multiple, and possibly conflicting, purposes at work in the activity?" In studying the social world of Catherine's family as a system, Sarah's students examined the question of the family's purpose or agenda—whether the family as a system functioned to subordinate women—particularly, resistant women such as Catherine—or to foster children's sense of autonomy and self-worth.

In studying characters' or people's roles, students might ask, "What roles or identities do participants or characters or people enact in a world? How do these roles or identities vary across different worlds? What practices or language do they employ to enact a role or identity? What are their feelings about being in a role or identity?" Sarah's students compared the roles of females in the medieval world with those of females in the contemporary world. They constructed a comparison chart listing aspects of the medieval world on one side and related aspects of the modern world on the other side. Pairings included the following: "rarely bathed / bathed often, one main religion / variety of religions, father finds a husband for daughter / father's approval is not necessary, but nice." Such pairings helped students understand that while women were particularly subordinated to men during the medieval period, such subordination sometimes continues in contemporary society.

In studying characters' or people's rules or norms that are considered to be appropriate, significant, or valid practices within a social world, students might ask: "What is considered to be appropriate versus inappropriate behavior? What rules does this suggest? Who do I [the student] see as following or not following these rules? What do these rules suggest about the type of world the characters inhabit?" Sarah's students noted that strict rules regarding women in Catherine's society were linked to rules operating in the Catholic Church.

In studying characters' or people's beliefs, students might ask: "What reasons do participants give for their practices in a world? How do these reasons reflect their beliefs about the practices operating in a certain world? How do my own beliefs shape my perceptions of or responses to a world?"

Sarah reported that her students identified some of the prevailing beliefs operating in the medieval period, beliefs that astounded them. She noted that they reacted negatively to the beliefs in forced marriages, the subordination of women, and the extent of control exercised by the Catholic Church. Making these beliefs explicit led students to reflect on how their own beliefs shaped their responses to the novel.

In studying the history of a social world, students examine the traditions and evolution of a past world that shapes the current world. In studying a family world, they may examine traditions of celebrating holidays or taking vacation trips. In studying a school world, they may examine traditions such as the prom, graduation and awards ceremonies, pep rallies, or orientation programs for new students. In studying a community world, they may study holiday celebrations, parades, carnivals, bazaars, festivals, and so on. In many cases these traditions are immune to change. For example, in Shirley Jackson's story "The Lottery," members of a small town engage in an annual ritual of selecting one person to stone to death.

In Kim's class, students were particularly interested in issues related to history. Having examined some of the myths shaping their perceptions of the American West, they recognized that myths could shape their perceptions of all of history, particularly in terms of understanding the role of the family in the 1950s and 1960s. As Kim noted, "They showed interest in talking about the 1960s—another decade that would be good to explore in terms of myth versus reality. The idea of history being anything other than chronological, factual, and 'true' seemed to be too much of a contradiction for them. . . . History is fact in school."

Representing and Mediating Social Worlds through Tools

Students may also study how characters use various tools—e.g., language, genres, discourses, signs—to represent or mediate their perceptions of social worlds within an activity system. By *mediate* I mean the way in which tools serve to connect the participant and the purpose within an activity or world (Vygotsky). Barbara Rogoff gives the example of selling Girl Scout cookies, in which the object of the activity is to sell as many cookies as possible. To achieve that object, Girl Scouts use tools including a sales pitch, charts, and ledgers. These tools serve to mediate the relationship between the activity's object of achieving high cookie sales and their roles as Girl Scouts. The meaning of these tools is constituted by how they are used to achieve an activity's object or purpose.

One example of a tool used to represent roles in a system is signs. People and characters use signs as social markers to represent their own allegiances to social worlds. The meaning of such a sign is defined by codes that consist of systems of signs and that assign meanings to the various signs within a given system (Peirce). Decoding a system within a social world thus means unpacking the meanings operating within a sign system. For example, adolescents in Britain have created their own system for using beepers to communicate to each other (Street). Based on a system of Morse code beeps, they can send messages to each other that are indecipherable by others. A sequence of beeps reading "121" on the digital display means "I want to talk to you alone."

In responding to S. E. Hinton's novel *The Outsiders*, John Moore noted the use of various signs: "the word *cool*, the cars that the Socs drive, the imagery of sunsets, and the way that Ponyboy Curtis slouches, his body language, are signs with which these two gangs socially construct themselves" (212). The two different gangs employ different signs—such as dress, language, and gestures—to represent two competing class worlds, each with its own codes. As Moore notes:

> Dress is a major sign in the novel that serves as a tool for expressing allegiance to a peer group or school social world. Ponyboy explains how the East Side (middle class) gang members code themselves: "We wear our hair long and dress in blue jeans and T-shirts, or leave our shirttails out and wear leather jackets and tennis shoes or boots" (6). . . . In contrast, the rich-kid Socials live on the privileged West Side. As four carloads of Socs arrive for the rumble, Ponyboy describes them: "They looked like they were all cut from the same piece of cloth: clean-shaven with semi-Beatle haircuts, wearing striped or checkered shirts with light-red or tan-colored jackets or madras ski jackets. They could just as easily have been going to the movies as to a rumble." (213)

In responding to *Catherine, Called Birdy*, Sarah's students examined the ways the novel represented an adolescent female during the medieval period. They questioned the degree to which she is a realistic depiction of an adolescent girl during this time period. Most believed that she was atypical, but they wondered if it was possible that an adolescent girl would feel and act this way during the Middle Ages. Students also discussed the representation of the father and the extent to which he had any redeeming qualities.

Kim's students examined various media representations of the West, the family, small towns, gender roles, and American Indians that perpetuate various myths about these worlds. One group of students studied idealized media representations of the small town as a pastoral world with no social or environmental problems. They critiqued these myths by examining the portrayal of crime in *Montana, 1948*. The novel's narrator, David, reveals how the townspeople deliberately admitted to various crimes: "From the eccentric to the unusual to the aberrant. From Scott and her palominos to Mrs. Russell, who was a kleptomaniac, to Arne Olsen, a farmer, who never bathed . . . to my Uncle Frank who molested his patient. How many secrets had our town agreed to keep?" (Watson 128).

Another group studied idealized representations of the model family on television programs such as *Father Knows Best* and *The Brady Bunch*. They then contrasted these idealized representations with more conflicted versions of the family portrayed in *Home Improvement, Married with Children,* and *Montana, 1948,* a novel in which the father, his brother, and their father are continually fighting.

Another group studied the stereotyped representation of American Indians in the film *Dances with Wolves,* which portrays American Indians as continually fighting wars against Whites. They explored how these representations shape the narrator David's perspective in *Montana, 1948* after his uncle kills Mary, an American Indian female. They are curious as to why the American Indians in the town do not seek revenge for Mary's death, something that would occur in a Hollywood movie.

Studying these media representations led students to recognize how their own perceptions of these novels were shaped by experiences with such media representations. They realized that their responses to Davy's father as sheriff in *Montana, 1948* were influenced by Hollywood stereotypes of the sheriff. They could then reflect critically on the limitations of their own preconceptions about character types, thus moving themselves to the next step in the process—critiquing.

In addition to studying about systems portrayed in literature, it is also the case that students are themselves responding within the context of school or classroom activities as systems. Within these activities they employ various tools—e.g., language, signs, narratives, genres, computers, writing, images, music, drama, mathematics, art, music, photography, video, computer graphics—to represent their responses to social worlds portrayed in literature and linked to their own lived-world experiences (Smagorinsky and O'Donnell). For example, high school students at State College Area High School, State College, Pennsylvania, constructed Web-based hypertext responses to stories about love, family, and peer relationships in the story collection *Coming of Age* (Emra). (See http://www.ed.psu.edu/k-12/teenissues.) They drew on their own lived-world experiences in peer and family relationships to interpret the relationships in these stories. They then used images, photos, video clips, or songs from their own lives or the media to define intertextual links between their own lives and the portrayals of characters' relationships.

Students in Kim's classes used collages to represent their perceptions of images of and texts about familial, Hollywood Western, small-town, and American Indian worlds. These collages reflected a range of conflicting representations of these worlds, from the stereotyped *Leave It to Beaver* or *Father Knows Best* idealization of the family to more realistic images of small town and American Indian life.

One useful tool for representing responses to literature is drama. Students can role-play or create skits dramatizing the concerns, issues, or dilemmas portrayed in texts. By adopting the roles of persons or characters coping with an issue or dilemma, students consider the moral effects of their actions on others who may not share their own beliefs. In these dramatizations, students "not only adopt positions; they encounter situations and points of view that challenge and change them and their views of whatever they are studying" (Wilhelm and Edmiston 6). For example, in one small-town school district, a group of parents has objected to the use of a controversial novel in a high school English class, filing a complaint with the high school principal and the school board. The students in one class created a role-play about the issue of censorship, adopting the roles of school board members, parents, and local organizations opposed to the use of the book, as well as parents in favor of it (Beach and Marshall). Students assuming these roles then testified about their responses to the book and their attitudes toward censorship, testimony the board considered when voting on a policy decision. Student proponents of censorship employed narratives, depicting instances of innocent students who were negatively influenced or "corrupted" by reading books.

At the end of the role-play, students stepped out of their roles and reflected on their use of tools to construct their roles and the world of the small-town school board meeting. For example, a student who assumed the role of a mother described her awkwardness in having to defend the need for censorship. By writing about their feelings, students grappled with differences between their own attitudes and those associated with their role.

Critiquing and Transforming Social Worlds

Based on their contextualization and analysis of representations, students then critiqued the limitations of the social worlds they were studying, critiques that led to suggestions for transforming those worlds. Students may be more motivated to engage in inquiry when they know that they have the power to critique and transform a social world. Sarah noted that her middle-school Girls' Book Club group was more engaged in the study of gender-role issues because they could both critique beliefs about gender roles and entertain ways of changing those roles.

In critiquing social worlds, students challenge or interrogate the common-sense, taken-for-granted assumptions underlying the construction or representation of a social world. Questioning what is considered to be "normal" or "real" in a social world involves perceiving the familiar as strange, which, in turn, involves suspending one's usual ways of perceiving or contextualizing a world and adopting an outsider's view or "Martian perspective." The Martian visitor knows nothing about the usual, accepted practices in a social world and is therefore in a position to question or challenge those practices. Adopting the perspective of a naive outsider means that a student is more likely to ask questions such as "Why are people doing this?" or "What is the purpose for this practice?"

After finishing work on *Catherine, Called Birdy*, pairs of students each identified a topic or issue related to women in present-day society: single-sex classrooms, women in the military, equal rights activism, women in sports and Title IX, mail-order brides, comparing women in different cultures, historical women, women during war, media representation of women, the "glass ceiling," and "super mom." One group, for example, studied the role of advertising related to body weight. They gathered data on and eventually critiqued the use of thin models in advertising to portray an unrealistic perception of body weight. The students then presented their findings to a group of sixth-grade females for the purpose of helping transform these sixth graders' beliefs about women's roles in society. Making these presentations served to bolster their own sense of self-efficacy as having expertise about women's roles. Students were encouraged to find ways that would actively involve the sixth-grade girls through games, discussions, opinion polls, video clips, PowerPoint presentations, and skits.

Kim's students critiqued the various forces operating within the family, small-town, and justice systems portrayed in *Montana, 1948*. They had prepared themselves for critiquing these systems through their previous critical analysis of Hollywood representations of the West. They critiqued, for example, the failure of family members to communicate with each other, as in the failure of the father in *Montana, 1948* to confront his brother about his treatment of women.

As part of their critiques, they noted the difficulty of attempting to transform a provincial, racist, small-town system in which close personal and family ties are at stake, dramatized in the father's difficulty in changing the system when the brother and grandfather are attempting to perpetuate the status quo. Students then proposed alternative ways to transform families who are coping with difficulties.

In summary, engaging in these various critical inquiry projects helped Sarah's and Kim's students purposefully construct and critique social worlds portrayed in literature as systems. Learning to use these strategies helps students develop greater understanding of how language serves as a tool for constructing these systems, an understanding essential for interrogating their own social worlds.

Works Cited

Beach, Richard, and James Marshall. *Teaching Literature in the Secondary School.* Belmont, CA: Wadsworth, 1991.

Beach, Richard, and Jamie Myers. *Inquiry-Based English Instruction: Engaging Students in Life and Literature.* New York: Teachers College P, 2001.

Bruner, Jerome. *Actual Minds, Possible Worlds.* Cambridge, MA: Harvard UP, 1986.

Cushman, Karen. *Catherine, Called Birdy.* New York: Clarion, 1994.

Edelsky, Carole. "On Critical Whole Language Practice: Why, What, and a Bit of How." *Making Justice Our Project: Teachers Working toward Critical Whole Language Practice.* Ed. Carole Edelsky. Urbana, IL: National Council of Teachers of English, 1999. 7–36.

Engeström, Yrjö. *Learning by Expanding: An Activity-Theoretical Approach to Developmental Research.* Helsinki: Orienta-Konsultit Oy, 1987.

Mellor, Bronwyn, and Annette Patterson. "Critical Practice: Teaching 'Shakespeare.'" *Journal of Adolescent and Adult Literacy* 43.6 (2000): 508–17.

Moore, John. "Street Signs: Semiotics, *Romeo and Juliet,* and Young Adult Literature." *Theory into Practice* 37.3 (1998): 211–19.

Mosenthal, Peter. "Reframing the Problems of Adolescence and Adolescent Literacy: A Dilemma-Management Perspective." *Reconceptualizing the Literacies in Adolescents' Lives.* Ed. Donna E. Alvermann, Kathleen A. Hinchman, David W. Moore, Stephen F. Phelps, and Diane R. Waff. Mahwah, NJ: Erlbaum, 1998. 325–52.

Peirce, Charles S. *Collected Papers of Charles Sanders Peirce.* Cambridge, MA: Harvard UP, 1931–58.

Phelan, Patricia, Ann Locke Davidson, and Hanh Cao Yu. *Adolescents' Worlds: Negotiating Family, Peers, and School.* New York: Teachers College P, 1998.

Rogoff, Barbara. "Observing Sociocultural Activity in Three Planes: Participatory Appropriation, Guided Participation, and Apprenticeship." *Sociocultural Studies of Mind.* Ed. James V. Wertsch, Pablo del Río, and Amelia Alvarez. New York: Cambridge UP, 1995. 129–64.

Russell, David. "Rethinking Genre in School and Society: An Activity Theory Analysis." *Written Communication* 14.4 (1997): 504–54.

Short, Kathy, and Jerome Harste. *Creating Classrooms for Authors and Inquirers.* 2nd ed. Portsmouth, NH: Heinemann, 1996.

Smagorinsky, Peter, and Cindy O'Donnell-Allen. "Reading as Mediated and Mediating Action: Composing Meaning for Literature through Multimedia Interpretive Texts." *Reading Research Quarterly* 33.2 (1998): 198–227.

Street, Brian. "Developing New Literacies." Unpublished paper. London: Kings College, 1998.

Vygotsky, L.S. *Mind in Society: The Development of Higher Psychological Processes.* Ed. Michael Cole, Vera John-Steiner, Sylvia Scribner, and Ellen Souberman. Cambridge, MA: Harvard UP, 1978.

Watson, Larry. *Montana, 1948: A Novel.* Minneapolis: Milkweed, 1993.

Wells, Gordon. *Dialogic Inquiry: Towards a Sociocultural Practice and Theory of Education.* New York: Cambridge UP, 1999.

Wilhelm, Jeffrey, and Brian Edmiston. *Imagining to Learn: Inquiry, Ethics, and Integration through Drama.* Portsmouth, NH: Heinemann, 1998.

12 Inquiry, Folkloristics, and Discussion: Unbinding Literature in the Classroom

Jacqueline S. Thursby
Brigham Young University

This chapter begins with definitions of terms used in the title which will be developed in the following pages.

Inquiry: "The National Research Council and the National Academy of Sciences define inquiry as 'a multifaceted activity that involves making observations; posing questions; examining books and other sources of information to see what is already known; planning investigations; reviewing what is already known in light of experimental evidence; using tools to gather, analyze, and interpret data; proposing answers, explanations, and predictions; and communicating the results'" (Routman 464).

Folkloristics: This term is used to describe methodologies utilized in the study of folklore. It is the study of expressive culture that emerges from various groups. *Folklore,* a term coined in the 1840s by English scholar W. J. Thoms, is an often misunderstood concept and discipline. More than simple stories of the folk, it is transmitted, creative, and traditional human behavior: that is, things people do, say, make, and believe—and often do not put in written form. Paul Bunyan and Pecos Bill are often present in collections of American folktales, and each forms a genuine part of American popular culture, but both were creations of imaginative professional writers. Instead of lived folklore, literary tales such as these are often called *fakelore.* That is a term coined by Richard Dorson to attack materials that he felt misrepresented traditional folklore ("Folklore and Fakelore" 335–43). In recent years, however, "American folklorists have begun to analyze even fakelore itself as a reflection of traditional culture" (Brunvand 6). Folkloristics, then, is both a discipline and a methodology "devoted to the identification, documentation, characterization, and analysis of traditional *expressive* forms, processes, and behaviors . . . (alternatively identified as folklore studies or folklife research)" (Georges and Jones 1, emphasis in original).

Discussion: This term is used here to indicate an informal consideration of an issue or topic in an open discussion setting or forum. Classroom discussion, both large-group and small-group, is an important educational tool, and by combining an inquiry-based strategy with folkloristics the teacher and students can be introduced to a different and easily understood approach to literary discussion. "As a leader of discussion, you have an obligation to respond to what you hear, not just what you want to hear. You need to be able to make connections when students may not be able to and to recognize significant points in their conversations to 'bridge' and open up other possibilities" (Graham, Hudson-Ross, Adkins, McWhorter, and Stewart 144).

Unbinding literature (or unbinding the text): A metaphor that I have coined, "to unbind the text" means to unravel or undo elements that may otherwise be bound so tightly in the prose that it is easily overlooked. A reader unfamiliar with folklore is likely to leave folkloric examples bound in the reading without realizing the richness of meaning that folklore often adds. The folkloristic approach to literature thus opens and unbinds often overlooked information and provides mutual discovery for both students and teachers. Authors construct nuances for readers. Sometimes meaning emerges from the writer's own experience and intertwines with the readers' lived experiences. Selection of folkloric expression helps the author shape meaning in individualistic ways; there are often rich cultural dimensions in a simple phrase or artifact which enhance the text immeasurably. Unbinding the meaning of traditional vernacular folklore leads the reader more deeply into connotations woven through the text. By carefully examining some of the lore used in the texts, we find concrete evidence with which we can more fully discern connections between ourselves and the author's possible narrative intentions.

What, then, is traditional, vernacular folklore? In short, it involves spoken customs and practices usually transmitted from person to person by word of mouth. Within the broad spectrum of expressive human behavior and culture, folklorists collect, classify, and analyze under the following basic categories: (1) oral—things people say, (2) material—things people make, (3) customary—things people do, and (4) belief—ideas people embrace. Some instances can be clearly defined and belong to only one category. Others, such as superstitions, can be categorized under more than one heading (in this case, oral and belief). Some items have fuzzy definitions, such as an old vernacular (oral)

With Their Words (Oral Lore)		With Their Hands (Material Lore)		With Their Actions (Customary Lore)
epics	names	houses	*Things:*	*Celebrations:*
ballads	autograph verses	barns	knitted	family
lyrics	limericks	fences	whittled	weddings
legends	epitaphs	tools	braided	birthdays
folktales	leave-takings	toys	sculpted	anniversaries
jokes	greetings	tombstones	stitched	funerals
riddles	tongue-twisters	foods	woven	holidays
proverbs	toasts	costumes	quilted	dances
chants	teases			instrumental music
charms	taunts			gestures
oaths	retorts			pranks
curses	insults			games

I would add the following as a fourth category:

With Their Minds
(Belief Lore)

superstitions
folk medicine
folk religion
religious traditions

Figure 1. Things people make . . .

recipe for mashed potato candy. Does the recipe fit under oral (for the directions) or material (for the candy)? William Wilson, recently retired folklorist from Brigham Young University, generated lists for three broad categories of folkloric items for a class handout (see Figure 1). He discussed these elements further in his article "Documenting Folklore" (225).

     Because of ambiguity in defining some of the items, it is helpful to remind students that it is sometimes necessary to guess at meaning: "What seems meaningless is full of hidden meaning if only you have the key" (Geertz 184). By looking at some of the beliefs or oral, material, and customary items used or portrayed in literature, and then reflecting on one's own possible knowledge and experience with those items, it is sometimes possible to discover meaningful keys to the author's intention. At one point in *To Kill a Mockingbird,* for instance, Scout explains what she saw from a tree house: "looking over the schoolyard, spying on multitudes of children through a two-power telescope Jem had given me, learning their games, following Jem's red jacket through wriggling circles of blind man's buff, secretly sharing" (Lee 15). For me, that passage invoked memories of my Missouri childhood and a family tree house I had not thought about for years. We climbed there to spy sometimes, and in the schoolyard we also played what we called "blindman's *bluff*." In this example, the memory of similar homespun experiences engaged my perception with the reality of Scout's context and made Lee's familiar episodes in the book even more meaningful to me. If a student responded with a similar memory in the classroom, a discussion of tree houses might take place, or a discussion of playground games, possibly engaging even the most reluctant student in the conversation.

On the other hand, authors also use metaphors, allusions, and folkloric information with seemingly obscure (to a given reader) or at least unfamiliar meanings. In *The Chosen*, for instance, references to the *Pirkei Avot*, "a collection of Rabbinic maxims . . . studied by many Jews every Shabbat between Passover and the Jewish New Year" (Potok 130), maxims used in their customary folkloric traditions, provoked no memory or understanding from my lived experience. Guessing at the author's usage and the meaning in the text opens up literary engagement and voicing in the classroom. It opens doors to the wonder of discovery. By unbinding overlooked folklore embedded in the texts, then, students learn to engage in critical inquiry and discussion.

Two important purposes of education are to help students learn to examine information and develop the ability to think critically by asking questions. They need to learn to negotiate their realities and experiences in a positive and reasonable way. Literature, both fiction and nonfiction, helps students to engage and critique the life choices of others through vicarious experience. Whole-class discussion and listening to one another in the classroom open paths to thinking and examination that can result in more refined methods of negotiation. By responding to the literature through a folkloristic lens, students can safely engage in the discussion, learn to inquire intelligently about how the text possibly has personal meaning in their lives, and willingly write their responses to the literary material because it has taken on a meaning related to their own experience. In the following pages, I have provided a background and foundation for a folkloric approach to literature, followed by consideration of methods for applying the theory to active classroom literary discussion and writing.

To use this approach, it is helpful for both teacher and students to understand a few of the more basic folkloric elements. Folk items and their meaning often change according to human need. Those variations on a theme are called *variants*. A quilt pattern that represents a certain meaning in 1800 may have the same or a different meaning in 2000.

Legends become localized; that is, essentially the same story about a ghost might be told in Bangor, Maine, or Albuquerque, New Mexico, with a different setting and characters. Jokes may be similar but have various protagonists and victims, and many basic recipes have a thousand variants. Folk medicine, religious customs, and even classroom behavior evolve and change. To share it; to talk about it; to collect, classify, and analyze it—this is folklore.

Two other important basic elements of folkloristics are *dynamic variation* and the *twin laws of folklore process*. *Dynamic variation* means that there can be many varieties or *variants* of the same folkloric item. To demonstrate this principle, Steve Siporin, a folklorist and professor at Utah State University, has students in his introductory classes of folklore make paper airplanes. The students produce a variety of paper creations and attempt to sail them toward a wastebasket in the front of the room. Some fly; some do not. Some hit the basket; most do not. The objective is to visually experience the concept of dynamic variation. Everyone makes an airplane, and no two planes are exactly the same— that is dynamic variation. The other basic elements, called the *twin laws of folklore process*, are conservatism and dynamism. Folklorist Barre Toelken explains:

> *Conservatism* refers to all those processes, forces, and attitudes that result in the *retaining* of certain information, beliefs, styles, customs, and the like, and the attempted passing of those materials, essentially intact through time and space, in all the channels of vernacular expression. . . . *Dynamism*, at the other extreme, comprises all those elements that function to alter features, contents, meanings, styles, performance, and usage as a particular traditional event takes place repeatedly through space and time. (39)

The basic item "paper airplane," a traditional child's toy, is the *conservative* element. The varied interpretations created by Siporin's folklore students constitute the *dynamic* element. The twin laws of folklore process would be demonstrated in dynamic variation, meaning that the conservative element (the airplane) and the dynamic element (the variations of the airplane) are both present in the concept of dynamic variation.

My interest in combining folkloric elements and literary discussion developed from secondary classroom observations made in my role as professor of secondary English methods and supervisor of student teachers and their mentors. Though many of my English student teachers are drawn to the profession because of their love of literature, they have asked for creative ways to engage their secondary students in meaningful literary discussion. In classroom visits, I have often noted that in-class reading time, and the associated discussion that follows, frequently lack enthusiasm. With some exceptions, fledgling and veteran teachers too often seem to be wading through classroom literary hours with minimal engagement. I was told that the books had to be read *in* the classroom because many secondary students wouldn't read at home, and further, if they did take the books home, the students had so little interest that the books were often misplaced and not returned. I thought that more personal interest in reading could be generated if a folkloristic method could be created, taught, and understood.

The specific genesis for my folkloric discussion method came during a secondary classroom reading of Irene Hunt's *Across Five Aprils*, a story with a Civil War setting. A student was rapidly reading aloud after the class was told that they had to finish the text that day because the test on it was scheduled for the next day. The student read a passage in the text about laughing at an inappropriate time and sped on, paragraph to paragraph, until another took over the reading. The passage in question was "The distant horizon blurred a little, and the birds' trills and the soft golden blanket of sunlight over the fields and orchards seemed out of place—like laughter in a church" (Hunt 187). My train of thought went something like this: there were probably few people in that classroom who had not laughed at an inappropriate time. Laughing, or trying to stifle a giggle in church or at some other designated quiet time and then telling stories about it would be an example of folklore from personal experience.

Even the most reticent students might remember a story about that kind of an incident. That, I thought, might be a nonthreatening way to get the students to respond to the literature from their own experience. Folkloric reader response! The students could look for various kinds of folklore (oral, material, customary, belief) in the texts, identify them, and talk about them. This method—developed over a few years of research and experimenting—would be meant to augment the study of other themes in the novels, and it would provide a clearly delineated framework on which to build whole-classroom conversation. I termed this method "unbinding the text," and students and student teachers who have tried it find it useful.

For example, one of my students applied the folkloristic method in her teaching of *The Canterbury Tales* by Geoffrey Chaucer. She emphasized material culture (things people make). She contextualized the period of the work using appropriate social and cultural history, discussed the uses and meanings of clothing described in the text, and then had her students draw their imagined versions of the various characters' clothing. As a writing assignment, the students compared and contrasted their chosen characters' clothing with contemporary versions of attire for similar uses. The unit culminated with student presentations of their work, and most of the presentations triggered lively discussions that speculated, in part, on why we wear what we do.

Now let me turn to the method. The teacher will need to spend a few class periods helping the students to understand the basic concepts and elements of folklore. Examples from both fiction and nonfiction can be used. Write headings of the basic folklore categories on the board: oral, material, customary, and belief. Give individual sheets to students with the same headings and a few examples listed beneath each one. Discuss the categories and examples, then let students brainstorm personal examples of various items under each of the headings. The various categories can be used as topics for journal entries, large- or small-group discussion, or short personal essays. Because the students find these concepts concrete and easy to grasp, the teacher might find students reluctant to close the discussion; most groups of students have many examples of each category that they would like to share. Sometimes they will name items that are difficult to categorize, and that is part of the challenge about meaning and use. When a general understanding of the concepts is reached, you are ready to apply it to literary discussion.

As a guest teacher this past winter in a local high school, I taught a unit on superstitions in *Huckleberry Finn* to a junior English class. Beginning with oral lore, I asked every student to give an example of a superstition he or she had encountered in personally lived experience. Every student participated and enthusiastically shared examples. An old and nearly forgotten story emerged and triggered lively discussion. Stored in the collective memory of several students who had been together in school since kindergarten was a horror tale about Bloody Mary. They explained that she was a ghost figure that could appear if a person said "Bloody Mary" in front of a mirror three times. In their second-grade year, the story had circulated and caused fear among them. The children became obsessed with the idea and were blaming every class member's illness and injury on the ghostly presence of Bloody Mary. Finally, the second-grade teacher took time to dispel the horror of the Bloody Mary threat by explaining it as a foolish superstition. The regular classroom teacher of the high school class told me afterwards that students who rarely participated in class discussion were engaged and contributing that day. The students and I talked about the power of superstition, and we then returned to examining and discussing oral and material examples in *Huckleberry Finn*. This kind of interactive exchange demonstrates the value of applying folkloric methodology to literary discussion.

If you try this method, begin by reading a book, possibly *To Kill a Mockingbird,* in class in assigned blocks or segments, either silently or orally, and have the students identify folkloric elements on their individual papers as they encounter them in the text. At a predetermined point, stop reading and begin to share the folkloric elements found in the text. Ask why students think the author used those particular examples of folklore. Talk about how the author incorporated the lore into the story. Have the students share items from their own lived experience that are similar to what they find in the text. The students usually enjoy looking for the folkloric motifs as they read, and they are enthusiastic in the sharing and discussion. The discussion will be lively, and the students will learn from one another.

This folkloric literary strategy can be expanded to useful student research based on a method for literature and folklore study designed by the late Richard Dorson, one of the doyens of American folklore research and theory. Dorson was concerned that too many published folklore and literature articles were shallow and inaccurate (Dorson, "Interpretation" 1–8). He felt that some scholars were only identifying folklore in texts and writing about it without understanding. The folkloric elements were easily teased out of texts; but the guesses at meaning were often not useful, and the discussions did not contribute significantly to the understanding of how and why the lore was used. Dorson suggested that clarification of the relationship between literature and folklore could be established by providing three kinds of evidence.

First, the reader should research the author's *biographical evidence* to determine whether the author had firsthand experience with the folklore used in the story. Second, the items of folklore in the text are to be considered *internal evidence* and must be faithful descriptions of legitimate folklore. Third, with *corroborative evidence,* the reader is to determine whether the folklore in the text was used appropriately. Dorson did not suggest that this procedure was always necessary, but he taught that this took the reader to a higher level of understanding about how and why the folklore was used in the text. I have often used the example with my students that if a Maypole is to be used in a text with a setting of, perhaps, the early 1920s in New Jersey, would that be an appropriate use of the folkloric tradition of the Maypole? Might it really have been used as a cultural artifact then?

Dorson's method takes the students into the book to find evidence of folklore *and* into the library to study biographical information about the author. Library research also includes finding the historical or contextual/social setting for corroborative evidence. Educated guesses at meaning and usage are fair. In the writing of their research, students are encouraged to share folkloric traditions and practices from their own experience which may be similar to those the author used. My students have occasionally used ideas and experiences in their writing that they have heard from other students in class. The view of literature through a folkloristic lens is rich and satisfying to the students and the teacher. It constructs discussion, both orally and in writing, with a semi-structured guideline and yet leaves great space for individual interpretation and expression. The following pages will give sample materials related to two popular secondary texts: *To Kill a Mockingbird* and *The Chosen*. The entries here are not all-inclusive of the lore present in the texts, but they will provide a framework from which to teach and guide the students.

Prompts and Questions

While using this process, there are many appropriate uses of the folkloric information found in the text. The following questions may be useful while learning to use the method.

Biographical Evidence

> Did the items you selected likely come from the author's experience? Explain why you think they did or did not.
>
> Why do you suppose the author chose to use the folkloric items he or she did?

Internal Evidence of Folklore

> What makes the item you chose to list an instance of folklore?
>
> Into which category does the item fit?
>
> Might it fit into more than one category? Why?
>
> Does it have both conservative and dynamic elements?
>
> Are there dynamic variations?

Corroborative Evidence

> What are the implications of the item in relation to the context of the paragraph in which you found it?
>
> Is the item used appropriately?
>
> Does the item help to enhance the narrative? Why or why not?
>
> Does the item help you to better understand your notion of the author's intent? Why or why not?
>
> Have you had personal experience with this item?

To Kill a Mockingbird

Harper Lee's classic was first published in 1960. It won the Pulitzer Prize for fiction in 1961, and the film version won multiple Academy Awards. It is a story of growing up in a small Southern town where gossip, rumors, legends, and superstition mold the cultural context of everyone who lives there. It is a story about human dignity, and the folkloric classroom discussions can include topics about morals and values, including the potential damaging consequences of gossip and false constructions about others.

Biographical Information

Nelle Harper Lee was born April 28, 1926, in Monroeville, Alabama, a small community founded as a White settlement after Andrew Jackson defeated the Creek Confederacy in 1814. The youngest of three children, she studied law at the University of Alabama but dropped out six months before completing her degree. Her plan was to become a writer, but to date *To Kill a Mockingbird* is the only novel she has written. She has written several short essays describing personal experiences.

Corroborative Evidence

Harper Lee denies that her novel is autobiographical, but there are many parallels between her life and the character of Scout. Lee's father, Coleman Lee, was a lawyer. Her mother's middle name was Finch, the family surname in the novel. The main characters in the text are three children; Lee was the youngest of three children in her family. The town of Maycomb in the novel is a small Alabama town about the same size as Monroeville where she was born. Another telling point is the fact that Scout says she doesn't want to be a lawyer but considers such things as nursing and aviation (229, 230), and Lee dropped out of law school and then worked for an airline for many years.

Folklore in *To Kill a Mockingbird*

Oral

"According to neighborhood legend . . ." (9)

Animal Lore: "sort of like making a turtle come out . . ." (14)

Saying: "until you climb into his skin and walk around in it" (30)

Southern naming: "Miss Maudie" (46)

Saying: "Jem walked on eggs" (61)

Saying: "but remember it's a sin to kill a mockingbird" (90)

Responsive singing: "Miraculously, on pitch, a hundred voices sang out Zeebo's words" (121)

Proverb: "He that cometh in vanity departeth in darkness" (159)

Proverb: "A merry heart maketh a cheerful countenance" (159)

Material

Tree house and rope ladders (15, 144, 264)

Crackling bread (29)

Snowman (64)

Lane cake (73)

Widow's walk (80)

Dog-trot hall (vernacular architecture) (99)

Black church decor (120)

Christmas basket (192)

Hooking a rug (223)

Customary

Southern custom: "Swept yard" (8)

Dining custom of using silver: "silver saucer" (24)

Christmas: "getting rid of the tree" (30)

Prank: "sat on a flag pole" (32)

Game: "strip poker" (54)

Christmas: "decorated the tree" (79)

Tradition: the seating at Christmas dinner (81)

Practice: caste system (131, 226)

Southern custom: porch culture

Hunting custom: "frog sticking without a light" (177)

Belief

Folk medicine: lye and turpentine (26)

Folk medicine: dose of magnesia (29)

Folk belief: "Old Testament pestilence" (42)

Folk belief: "Footwashers" (44)

Belief system: "Voo-doo System" (103)

Belief system: "Ku Klux . . . sheets" (147)

Superstition (also oral): "'Angel-bright. Life-in-death; get off the road, don't suck my breath.' That keeps 'em from wrapping around you—" (37)

Superstition: "Haints, Hot Steams, incantations, secret signs . . ." (254)

Belief system: "Mennonites" (156)

The Chosen

Set in the tiny community of Williamsburg in Brooklyn, Chaim Potok's novel offers insight into the richness of Jewish tradition and heritage. It is a story about two fathers and their sons, one set belonging to the Hasidic Orthodox sect of Judaism, and the other embracing Conservative Judaism, a less restrictive form of the Jewish faith. It is a compelling narrative that gently examines conflict and wisdom with strength and grace. Like *To Kill a Mockingbird*, it is a story of dignity and truth. Those who have taught this book know that "readers of Chaim Potok's *The Chosen* don't learn everything about Hasidic Jews, but they know a lot more than they did before they read the book, and their interest may have been piqued so that they will continue to watch for information and to read other books" (Donelson and Nilsen 315).

Biographical Information

Potok was born in 1929 in the Bronx section of New York City. The oldest of four children, he graduated *summa cum laude* from Yeshiva University in 1950 with a B.A. in English literature. As the biography in one edition of *The Chosen* states, "He then received a rabbinic ordination in 1954 from the Jewish Theological Seminary of America. Dr. Potok, a member of the faculty of the University of Judaism in Los Angeles, spent a year in Israel completing his doctoral dissertation in philosophy from the University of Pennsylvania in 1965. He has written numerous articles, reviews, and stories, and in May 1966 he became editor of the Jewish Publication Society of America. *The Promise,* a sequel to *The Chosen*, was published in 1969" (Potok 272).

Corroborative Evidence

The author was born in New York City, and the story was set there in a time contemporary with the author's. The story is about Orthodox Hasidic Jews and non-Hasidic Jews and reflects a rich knowledge of eastern European Jewish traditions and language. Potok, whose parents were Jewish immigrants from Poland, was intimately familiar with those traditions. He suffered criticism from his parents, his Talmud teachers, and his peers because writing fiction was considered a less than worthy way to spend one's time. As do the characters in *The Chosen*, Potok has demonstrated his deep commitment to both scholarship and Judaism.

Folklore in *The Chosen*

Oral

Language: Yiddish—a Germanic language variety developed in Central and Eastern Europe (16)

Taunt: "Burn, you apikorsim!" (29)

Nickname: "side-curled fringe wearers" (38)

Saying: "I hit the canvas so hard I rattled my toenails" (42)

Quotation from *The Zohar* (91)

Legend (101)

Recitation: "the Scholar's Kaddish" (134)

Storytelling (187)

Material

Clothing of the Hasids (9, 14)

Black skullcap (32)

Teffilin and prayer book (56)

Talmud: Kiddushin (commentary) (68)

Shabbat (Sabbath) table (86)

Chicken soup (93)

Hairstyle: "braided bun" (94)

Foods (94, 117)

Synagogues: "Shtibblach" (108)

"eight-branched candelabrum" (116)

Customary

Varied customs (9)

Sports participation (11)

Eating with hat on (45)

Traditional selection of leaders (81)

Shabbat tradition (96)

Marriage traditions (102)

Gematriya (traditional game) (128)

Family traditions (130–31, 162)

Death tradition (241)

Belief

Ba'al Shem Tov: "God-invested personality" (9)

Folk belief (100)

Folk medicine (103)

"Havdalah, the brief service that marks the end of the Shabbat" (135)

Ordination (112)

Head nodding (120)

Smicha: Rabbinic ordination (246)

Bar Mitzvah (250)

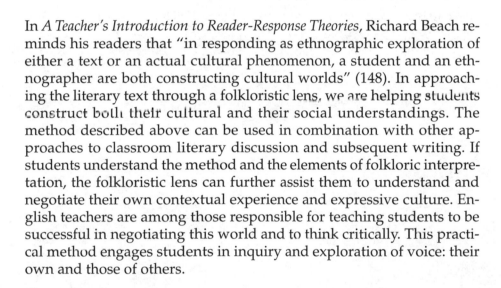

In *A Teacher's Introduction to Reader-Response Theories*, Richard Beach reminds his readers that "in responding as ethnographic exploration of either a text or an actual cultural phenomenon, a student and an ethnographer are both constructing cultural worlds" (148). In approaching the literary text through a folkloristic lens, we are helping students construct both their cultural and their social understandings. The method described above can be used in combination with other approaches to classroom literary discussion and subsequent writing. If students understand the method and the elements of folkloric interpretation, the folkloristic lens can further assist them to understand and negotiate their own contextual experience and expressive culture. English teachers are among those responsible for teaching students to be successful in negotiating this world and to think critically. This practical method engages students in inquiry and exploration of voice: their own and those of others.

Works Cited

Beach, Richard. *A Teacher's Introduction to Reader-Response Theories.* Teacher's Introduction Series. Urbana, IL: National Council of Teachers of English, 1993.

Brunvand, Jan Harold. *The Study of American Folklore: An Introduction.* 4th ed. New York: Norton, 1998.

Donelson, Kenneth L., and Alleen Pace Nilsen. *Literature for Today's Young Adults.* 5th ed. New York: Addison Wesley Longman, 1997.

Dorson, Richard M. "Folklore and Fakelore." *American Mercury* 70 (1950): 335–43.

———. "The Identification of Folklore in American Literature." *Journal of American Folklore* 70 (1957): 1–8.

Geertz, Clifford. *The Interpretation of Cultures.* New York: Basic, 1973.

Georges, Robert A., and Michael Owen Jones. *Folkloristics: An Introduction.* Bloomington: Indiana UP, 1995.

Graham, Peg, Sally Hudson-Ross, Chandra Adkins, Patti McWhorter, and Jennifer McDuffie Stewart, eds. *Teacher/Mentor: A Dialogue for Collaborative Learning.* New York: Teachers College P, 1999.

Hunt, Irene. *Across Five Aprils.* New York: Berkley, 1986.

Lee, Harper. *To Kill a Mockingbird.* New York: Warner, 1982.

Potok, Chaim. *The Chosen.* New York: Random, 1990.

Routman, Regie. *Conversations: Strategies for Teaching, Learning, and Evaluating.* Portsmouth, NH: Heinemann, 2000.

Toelken, Barre. *The Dynamics of Folklore.* Logan, UT: Utah State UP, 1996.

Wilson, William A. "Documenting Folklore." *Folk Groups and Folklore Genres: An Introduction.* Ed. Elliott Oring. Logan, UT: Utah State UP, 1986.

Part III Strategies for Assessing Inquiry-Based Approaches

13 Learning to Listen: Assessing Talk about Literature

Barbara G. Pace
University of Florida

Jane S. Townsend
University of Florida

Though most teachers value discussions of literature, class discussions can result in strikingly different experiences for students. In some contexts, literature discussions can alienate students from the processes needed to develop literary understandings, while in others they can deepen students' understandings of literature and improve their reading and writing. When discussions are effective, students connect with texts, ask probing questions, and negotiate the contradictory nature of literary meanings. Because class discussions can have such varying results, it is important to explore how discussions unfold in classrooms.

As teacher educators we have undertaken such explorations. In fact, we have spent the last several years thinking about and studying class discussions so that we might support engaging and worthwhile discussions with our own students. We have listened to classroom teachers talk about discussions in their classes, and we have encouraged prospective teachers to use discussion as a way of helping students relate to literature and to become more active readers. These experiences have taught us how difficult it is for any teacher to explore the nature of discussion in her or his own classroom. In this chapter, we share strategies for assessing the effectiveness of class discussions.

The Process of Assessing Discussion

Assessing class discussion begins by deciding what we want to know—that is, what we want to learn about the process of discussion or the results of discussion. Usually our questions come from discussions themselves. That is, some element of discussion catches our attention and fuels our curiosity. We may, for example, notice that students respond more readily to some topics than to others. We may have a particularly difficult time getting students to participate on a specific day and wonder why. Similarly, we may find ourselves in the midst of a particularly engaging discussion and wonder how we might keep the energy going or have a similar experience in another class. We may simply want to know how discussion, which is sometimes difficult and time consuming, functions as a teaching tool.

Other teachers may ask similar questions. For example, they may determine that they want to evaluate how they are responding to students. They might want to consider whether or not they are prompting students to provide evidence, to consider conflicting opinions, or to connect with what other students say. Teachers may want to learn more about the students in discussion. They may be curious about what connections students make, whether or not they demonstrate that they understand texts beyond a literal level, or what themes emerge in the discussions of different works.

Once a question or area of focus has been selected, a record of the discussion must be made so that the discussion can be assessed, and this can be done in two primary ways: (1) making a video or audio recording or (2) taking notes as the discussion unfolds in class. Obviously, preserving the discussion on audio- or videotape gives the most complete record of a discussion. When preserved in this way, a discussion can be transcribed to form a co-constructed, collaborative text that provides snapshots of classroom life. Such a text can be read to explore the patterns and strategies that emerge. However, producing such a document can be time consuming.

Thus, though verbatim transcripts of discussion texts are useful, many teachers do not create them. Rather, they adopt strategies that allow them to keep track of participants' ideas and exchanges as the discussion unfolds in their class. For example, Andrasick photocopied a seating chart and recorded ideas that arose as her eleventh-grade students discussed texts. As the students talked, these notes helped her link students' comments to one another. Making such connections with her students helped her demonstrate how they might consider one another's perspectives to gain deeper understandings of literature. After the discussion concluded, she referred to the notes she had made on the seating chart to summarize students' contributions and to reflect on "the pattern of a discussion" (27). By considering discussion in this way, she was able to evaluate student progress and to plan future classes and activities.

In another eleventh-grade classroom, Standiford assigned pairs of students to watch two film versions of *Hamlet* and discuss the films by comparing them on a variety of points. Students were required to audiotape their discussions and submit the tapes. She listened to the tapes to monitor students' development of literary knowledge. At the end of the academic year, she required students to listen to these tapes, as well as to other tapes they had made throughout the year, and to assess their own growth and development. Other teachers make video recordings of class discussion or ask students to serve as recorders. Some teachers simply stop a discussion in progress to call for a group assessment of what ideas have surfaced or what ideas are not being expressed. Such tactics provide a way for teachers to help students focus on the dynamics of discussion so that students may both understand and participate in the process.

Other strategies that may be used to create a discussion text include tracing the evolution of a single issue as it is addressed in class. For example, to understand how students think about different literary characters, teachers can make a chart and quickly add comments during the ongoing discussion. To collect information in this way, a teacher might place each character's name at the top of a column. As students talk, teachers can jot down bits of what is said or simply record a positive (+) or a negative (-) symbol beneath the name of the character being discussed. Later, this chart can be used to help students consider writing topics or to engage students in thinking about their own responses to the actions and motives of characters.

Evaluating the "Text" or the Process of a Discussion

Once a discussion has been captured, either by recording it or by taking notes, it should be evaluated. Going over the notes of the discussion or replaying discussion tapes can help teachers explore their questions about the discussion.

As addressed above, teachers can also evaluate discussions as they happen. One way to do this is by creating a chart, such as the one shown in Figure 1. This chart can be used to evaluate how discussion supports students as they develop literary understandings and strategies for interpreting and making sense of literature. And it can be used to help teachers determine how students are learning in a discussion and what role discussions are playing in the overall curriculum. During discussion, the chart can be used as a checklist for marking student behaviors and responses. Each element in the chart is explained below.

1. Students seek understanding in collaboration with others.	
2. Students ask questions about the text.	
3. Students refer to the text for support.	
4. Students refer to the ideas or words of others.	
5. Students make connections with texts and between texts.	

Figure 1. Chart for assessing student learning during a discussion.

1. Students seek understanding in collaboration with others. This behavior is evident when students are dealing with ambiguity in a text, such as trying to understand a character's motive for a specific action. For example, when studying *Hamlet*, students may grapple with the motivation of the ghost of Hamlet's father. They may wonder whether or not he is an honest ghost. Several students may participate in trying to reach a conclusion about the nature of the ghost. As they do so, they engage in problem solving by looking at the textual evidence available and by considering each other's ideas.

2. Students ask questions about the text. Generally, students ask two kinds of questions about texts: (1) information-seeking questions and (2) wondering questions (Townsend, 1993). When students ask the first kind of question, they are trying to clarify their understanding of the literal story. For example, a student may need to know the relationship between Ophelia and Polonius in order to understand deeper issues in the play. Students and teachers can also ask wondering questions; they may wonder whether or not Gertrude is complicitous in the murder of King Hamlet, a question that has no definitive answer. Both wondering and information-seeking questions are valuable as students learn the processes of appreciating and accepting the ambiguities inherent in literature.

3. Students refer to the text for support. When students are trying to answer a question about the text or deal with textual ambiguity, they can refer to the text for support. For example, when a student asks a question about Hamlet's sanity, he or she might cite his erratic behavior with Ophelia, and another student might cite Horatio's concerns about Hamlet. These actions demonstrate that students understand that the text is the source they must return to for further information. Learning this strategy is a key to developing textual competence.

4. Students refer to the ideas or words of others. As students participate in discussion, they can demonstrate their discussion skills by listening and responding to each other and to the teacher. For example, if
one student asks whether or not Gertrude had a choice in her marriage
to Claudius, other students may pick up this idea and wonder about
the possibilities it offers. One student might suggest that Hamlet thinks
she had a choice, and another student might argue that marrying
Claudius was the only way that Gertrude could remain queen. In this
way, students' ideas become incorporated into one another's thinking
about the text.

5. Students make connections with texts and between texts. As students talk about a text, they may connect what is happening in the text
with items or actions that are familiar to them. The connections between
texts can help them understand all texts more deeply. In trying to understand the nature of the ghost of Hamlet's father, for example, students may note that he faded when the light came. They may connect
the ghost's fear of light with a sign of evil by calling on their memories
of horror movies or vampire tales. Gaining an understanding of
intertextuality, of the relationships between texts, is an important aspect of developing as a reader of literature. Furthermore, connecting
with texts on a personal level demonstrates that students are connecting with the story world and learning that texts have personal meanings related to their own lives.

Much of what is good about classroom discussion is based on a
teacher's response to students' talk about texts and on the context for
learning that he or she has established in the classroom. By using the
chart above, or developing a chart that fits her or his own questions, a
teacher can consider the kinds of literary understandings that are developing as students talk about texts and can assess how literature instruction is working in the class. Such measures can help justify the use
of class discussion as a mechanism for helping students understand that
texts have meaning and make sense.

Helping students reach this understanding is important because
many students do not grasp this basic concept about literary texts. Standardized tests and the emphasis on basal reading and phonics have left
many students with the idea that reading is only about the pronuncia-
tion of words and that responding to texts is about filling in blanks. Students whose reading history has emphasized word calling are not likely
to understand that reading involves making meaning. Teachers can help

students gain this insight by creating discussions in which students are taught to use the strategies described here to construct meanings. This approach can also help students work toward a genuine engagement with literary texts, whereas students who do not understand that reading is about creating meaning will be lost when presented with complex works, and they will be uninterested, perhaps even unable to participate, in the exchange of ideas in group discussion.

Conclusion

By capturing and reading discussion texts, or by exploring discussions on the fly, teachers can assess how discussion is working in their classrooms and in what ways individual students are developing textual competence. Perhaps one of the greatest benefits, however, is that such explorations slow down text consumption (Scholes); that is, they encourage us to stop and examine the ways that words and meanings get shaped and lived. While such explorations are time consuming, they are important. Once we have glimpsed the complexities of discussion and considered how they help students learn, it is difficult to ignore those complexities. Furthermore, learning to listen to the evolution of ideas and the depth and breadth of student contributions can lead us as teachers to be more responsive to students, more capable of teaching them strategies for approaching texts, and more likely to help them value their ideas and their own capacity to think.

Works Cited

Andrasick, Kathleen D. *Opening Texts: Using Writing to Teach Literature.* Portsmouth, NH: Heinemann, 1990.

Scholes, Robert. *Textual Power: Literary Theory and the Teaching of English.* New Haven: Yale UP, 1985.

Standiford, Denise. "Gertrude as a Question." Annual Convention of the National Council of Teachers of English. Detroit. 21 Nov. 1997.

Townsend, Jane S. "Wondering Discourse in the Classroom." ERIC Document Reproduction Service No. ED 370 137, 1993. (Paper originally presented at the Annual Convention of the National Council of Teachers of English. Pittsburgh. Nov. 1993.)

14 Seminars and Self-Assessment

Burt Plumb
Indiana University South Bend

John N. Ludy
Fremont High School, Fremont, Indiana

We teach in a contradictory age. On the one hand, society bemoans our students' lack of originality, and business leaders challenge us to develop our students' abilities to think "outside the box." On the other hand, our state legislatures mandate standardized, high-stakes tests and graduation standards that push us and our students toward ever narrower expectations. Since financial incentives and punishments are often attached to these tests, it is hardly surprising that school administrators increasingly call for statistical evidence that classroom practices result in better academic performance as defined by the dictates of legislators, educational testing mavens, and state departments of education.

Faced with this confusing tug-of-war, many teachers have despaired. Some simply "teach to the test," replacing thoughtful explorations of relevant material with the trivial teaching of lists. Others have left teaching altogether. But in Indiana, increasing numbers of teachers have discovered Socratic seminars.

What is the result of this discovery? Walking into a classroom utilizing Socratic seminars, one immediately sees significant differences from the traditional classroom model. Rows and aisles are replaced by a geometric arrangement in which eye contact between each class participant is possible. Knowledge and understanding are constructed by the learners rather than received from the instructor. Learning is emergent, uncertain, and subject to revision. It is connected to what learners already know and is best created by cooperative action rather than by the teacher's or a student's solitary efforts. Students can be observed practicing the close reading of challenging texts. Participants build a community of learners based on a set of critical dialogue skills. They learn to demonstrate collegiality, which allows participants to reveal a vulnerability that leads to greater openness in the discussion and in turn accommodates a greater diversity of perspectives. Participants learn that at times they can be playful, and this promotes synergy within their conversations. The idea is to encourage "win/win" situations in which a community of learners nurtures each individual's development.

Initially, at Fremont High School, where I (John Ludy) teach, English teachers tried to incorporate at least one Socratic seminar per week in each class. We quickly recognized the seminar's power to challenge our students to explore, to inquire, and to think deeply. One by-product was an increased civility between all participants. Seminars also reduced time spent on discipline and class management. Students were attentive and engaged, and they were encouraged to seek further information outside the class. Teachers' respect for and recognition of students' abilities were also nurtured.

In the seminar format, as students' curiosity is piqued, their emergent questions tend to be of several types:

- clarification (e.g., What do you mean when you say_____?)
- probing of assumption (e.g., When you say _____, you seem to be assuming _____. Do I understand you correctly?)
- probing of reasons of evidence (e.g., How do you know?)
- questions about viewpoints and perspectives (e.g., What's an alternative?)
- probing of implications and consequences (e.g., What effect would that have?)
- questioning of the question (e.g., Why is this question important?)

As the students grapple with a variety of texts (short stories, poems, magazine or newspaper articles, Web site materials, art reproductions, musical selections, government documents, charts/graphs/statistics, grammar rules), the community's dialogue unfolds, and certain behaviors become evident. Students look toward each other when speaking rather than toward the teacher. Students make eye contact with whoever is speaking. They use the phrases "I think," "I agree," and "I disagree." Students simply wait their turn to speak rather than raising their hands for permission to talk. Students attribute ideas to one another by name. They use humor, and intellectual risk taking is commonplace. Students begin to form their own benchmarks and assess their own performances.

The Seminar: How to Prepare a Class

Pre-Course Assessment

On the first day of any course, Fremont High School's English teachers ask students to complete what we call the Pre-Course Assessment (see Figure 1). It is intentionally short and narrative, but it is valuable. If it is important for teachers to intimately know their students in order to teach them more effectively, the Pre-Course Assessment allows them to begin this voyage.

Because we also use student portfolios, this assessment will later be combined with the Seminar Response Sheet and the Post-Course Assessment (both addressed below). When these materials are considered together, students can intelligently assess their individual seminar learning experiences in the course.

Seminar Response Sheet

Since this will be the basis of individual assessment throughout the course, we spend some time going over it with students on the first day of a new class (see Figure 2).

1. Once students have finished the seminar reading, they will individually complete items 1 and 2.

   a. For Item 1 it is not necessary that we understand the exact meaning of every word. Rather, we should concentrate on the meanings of those words we must know to understand the gist of the reading.

   b. Students are advised that Item 2 is of particular interest because we teachers will shamelessly steal their questions for use in future seminars.

2. Students are then told that they will individually fill out the remainder of the seminar response sheet *after* the seminar is completed. Some of the more compulsive students will find this burdensome, but patience is one of many skills we are working on in seminars.

   a. For items 3 and 4, students should describe the text and the seminar using adjectives. They should then give their reasoning as to why these words best describe their experience.

   b. Item 5 accounts for half of each student's individual score for any seminar. (The other half is based on their thoughtful completion of the remainder of the response sheet.) It is their responsibility to honestly assess their individual performance.

Pre-Course Assessment

Name _____ Date _____ Course _____

1. Do you feel comfortable speaking in class? YES NO (Circle one)

   Why? _____

   _____

2. Do your classmates listen to what you say? YES NO

   Why? _____

   _____

3. Are the group projects worthwhile? YES NO

   Why? _____

   _____

4. Are the class discussions about the assignments worthwhile? YES NO

   Why? _____

   _____

5. Can you effectively analyze something you've read? YES NO

   Why? _____

   _____

6. Have you enjoyed this subject in the past? YES NO

   Why? _____

   _____

Figure 1

Seminar Response Sheet

Seminar Number: _____

Student Name: _____

Date: _____

Text Title and Creator: _____

Seminar Preparation

1. Are there any terms or phrases we need to explore?

2. What question(s) might we consider?

Seminar Reflections

3. The text was _____ because _____

_____

4. The seminar was _____ because _____

_____

5. On a scale of 1 to 10, I deserve a(n) _____ because _____

_____

6. On a scale of 1 to 10, _____ deserves a(n) _____ because _____

_____

7. The most interesting thing said today with which I agree was _____

_____

8. The most interesting thing said today with which I disagree was_____

_____

9. A good related topic we might want to explore is _____

_____

10. I connected today's topic with _____

_____

Figure 2

c. Items 6, 7, and 8 all help students build the ability to listen well. Further, they help students develop willingness to consider divergent viewpoints.

d. Items 9 and 10 challenge students to make meaningful connections. Students usually find these to be the hardest items to do; however, they often spur students to explore outside the classroom setting.

This may sound like a rather long presentation, but it really isn't. Usually, the entire explanation takes about ten minutes. We then immediately begin our first seminar.

Guidelines for Socratic Seminar Participants

Early in the year we hold a Socratic seminar concerning guidelines for seminar participants; students consider a previous class's guidelines and formulate their own (see Figure 3 for a sample set of guidelines). This seminar serves a three-fold purpose.

1. It helps make students better aware of what is expected of them in seminar and, consequently, gives them a better idea of how to accurately self-assess their individual performances.

2. It helps to further build a spirit of inquiry, cooperation, group responsibility, and openness. This is crucial to the transformation of any class into a community of learning.

3. It helps the teacher better understand the unique, emerging personality of each particular class section.

Students are provided with an individual copy of the guidelines to be used during the remainder of the school year. In addition, the guidelines are posted prominently on a classroom bulletin board as a constant reminder of our expectations. These are especially useful when we are reflecting at the end of a seminar or when the students are doing their self-assessments.

Portfolio Usage as an Element in Authentic Final Assessment

Students in Fremont's English classes use a three-file portfolio system. One of the files is specifically for graded seminar materials. Each seminar response sheet is filed in numerical order as it is returned.

As part of students' individual final exams, they are asked to write an essay summarizing their own seminar performances and experiences. As part of this essay, each student is asked to assign himself or herself an exam grade and turn it in with the portfolio's seminar file. Students understand that this grade is contingent on the quality of their essay

---

Guidelines for Socratic Seminar Participants

1. Refer to the text when needed during the discussion. A seminar is not a test of memory. You are not "learning a subject"; you are aiming at understanding ideas and issues.

2. It's OK to "pass" when asked to contribute, but chronic silence hurts the entire group.

3. Do not participate if you are not prepared. This is not a bull session.

4. Do not stay confused; ask for clarification.

5. Stick to the point; make notes about ideas you want to come back to.

6. Don't raise your hand; just wait your turn.

7. Speak up, so that all can hear you.

8. Listen carefully.

9. Talk to one another, not just to the teacher.

10. You are responsible for the seminar, even if you don't know it or admit it.

11. Assess yourself.

Figure 3

and its accompanying file. Rubrics used in our state's standardized essay test segments are utilized. Organization of this file consists of the following:

1. Pre-Course Assessment
2. Seminar Response Sheets in numerical order
3. Post-Course Assessment

Post-Course Assessment

After the last seminar in the course has been completed, students are asked to review their complete seminar portfolio file and complete the Post-Course Assessment (see Figure 4). As noted earlier, this final assessment is one part of the students' final exam.

The Post-Course Assessment provides teachers with an accurate and invaluable review of the seminar process in their classroom. As such, it should be closely read and reflected on.

Post-Course Assessment

Name _____ Date _____

1. Do you feel more comfortable speaking in public now than you did at the beginning of this course? YES NO (Circle one)
   Why? _____
   _____

2. Do your classmates listen to what you have to say? YES NO
   Why? _____
   _____

3. After reviewing your portfolio materials, indicate one thing that has changed in your
   a. writing: _____
   _____

   b. speaking: _____
   _____

   c. reading: _____
   _____

   d. listening: _____
   _____

   e. thinking: _____
   _____

4. What are you most proud of about your overall Socratic seminar experience?
   _____
   _____

5. Did your writing skills improve, stay the same, or decline? (Circle one)
   Why? _____
   _____

6. Did your speaking skills improve, stay the same, or decline?
   Why? _____
   _____

7. Did your reading skills improve, stay the same, or decline?
   Why? _____
   _____

8. Did your listening skills improve, stay the same, or decline?
   Why? _____
   _____

9. Did your thinking skills improve, stay the same, or decline?
   Why? _____
   _____

10. Would you recommend this course to other students? Yes No (Circle one)
    Why? _____
    _____

11. What are some advantages of Socratic seminars as a method of learning?
    _____
    _____

Thanks for sharing these responses.

Figure 4

The Seminar: A Typically Atypical Day

What does all this mean in an actual classroom setting? Let's consider a recent example. It is the fall semester, and my (John Ludy's) Block IV English 9 class consists of twenty-eight students. Since our school does not track, the students' grade performances range from A+ to F. We have two students repeating this course as sophomores. Several of the students have very low standardized test scores in language, and at least five of them have been suspended for various disciplinary reasons thus far this semester. All in all, it's a pretty typical public school class.

Since it's a Monday, we have several pieces of class business to take care of before we can begin the seminar. We deal with returned homework, the new vocabulary list, and general class announcements. Then students are given copies of an article by Washington Post reporter DeNeen L. Brown called "A Boy's Single Shot Spurs Endless Questions of Justice." The article examines the shooting of Kayla Rolland by a fellow first-grade student in Mount Morris, Michigan.

Next, students receive the day's Seminar Response Sheets. After they number this as seminar 13, they quietly read the article and complete the first two items on the response sheet.

When it's clear that the students have completed the reading, we begin to explore any words or terms about which they were uncertain. Students bring up three. Each time a new word or term is brought up, students are asked to read the sentence to gain context for the word. Then other students are asked to help give a definition. This day students figure the words out pretty easily. As a matter of fact, the term "felony" leads one of the kids to explain his own firsthand knowledge of the difference, at least in the state of Michigan, between a misdemeanor and a felony.

Once we have checked for problem words and phrases, I ask the seminar question: Why did this boy do what he did? Forty minutes later, students are still poring over the text to back up their answers. We have dealt with several possible, often diametrically opposed, viewpoints in a relatively civil and nonjudgmental manner. There's no way to summarize the many points students have raised or the many questions they have asked one another. The facilitator (who was, in this case, myself) has spent most of the time simply restating what students have said and acknowledging the next student who wants to speak. Likewise, he has occasionally taken notes about what's been said, simply because every typically atypical seminar is a learning experience for both the instructor and the students. For example, in this particular seminar, one student called attention to the fact that this boy was said to have lived in a "crack house," although no "crack" had been found when the police raided it.

Just as a student makes a particularly enlightening reference to the role of child protective services in this tragedy, the facilitator stops the seminar. Several students protest that they want to keep going. (This is a good sign, since one seminar goal is to encourage students to continue their dialogue outside of the classroom.) Participants are then asked a reflection question.

The reflection phase of a seminar concentrates on the process and *not* on the material. In other words, students are asked their impressions of what just happened. There is no single, standard reflection question any more than there is one standard seminar. One reflection question we have used is the following: What was an idea expressed today that you found particularly interesting, and who said it?

The facilitator then flips through a deck of cards with the students' names on them and asks for their reflections. The students think deeply about the question and the teacher learns quite a bit from their responses. Every student question is noted in the teacher's seminar journal; the most promising are marked for future use.

After completing this reflection activity, I remind students that the Seminar 13 Response Sheet is due tomorrow. Then we stop for the day.

At the beginning of the next day, I grade the response sheets during my prep period. Grading them is easy since the scoring is based on their own score plus one point for every completed item. More important, in grading them the facilitator gets valuable feedback that helps him or her rate the usefulness of the text for the future, as well as seminar strengths and weaknesses and related texts that might be explored.

Based on student reflections and response sheets, this text grades out as a B+. It was effective, but it will lose its immediacy rapidly. It is interesting that several students have made a connection to child abuse and neglect. Perhaps a future seminar with Theodore Roethke's "My Papa's Waltz" or the Marjorie Kinnan Rawlings short story "A Mother in Mannville" might work.

The next day, students receive their Seminar Response Sheets and file them in their individual portfolios. At the end of the semester, they will be asked to write an essay reviewing their seminar performance, and these response sheets will be needed at that time.

We believe this combination of assessments, response sheets, modified guidelines, portfolio files, and final test assignments helps students become more inquisitive, more reflective, more connected, and more self-motivated. Furthermore, it provides teacher-facilitators with statistical proof that seminars are not a "feel-good" waste of instructional time. In an educational climate of high-stakes standardized tests, such proof is often crucial.

It is also important to note that our data indicate that, when taken overall, student self-assessment scores are quite accurate. Table 1 compares teacher-graded composition assignments with student self-assessed seminar assignments in three different first-year English classes.

As you can see, the results are almost identical. Students' self-assessed scores were not inflated as compared to those given by the teacher. Similarly, turn-in rates were consistent for both. Clearly, teachers can safely turn over some of their assessment burdens to students and the sky will not fall.

Student self-assessment offers several advantages. First, it lightens teachers' grading loads and allows teachers more time to prep for classes. It is also a potent and neglected tool of inquiry. After all, evaluation is the highest level of Bloom's Taxonomy. When students are challenged to assess their own performances, they must internally inquire about their own definitions of quality and excellence. Rather than passively accepting or rejecting what they perceive as arbitrary measurements of their performance, they must articulate their own standards.

Thus, self-assessment fits well with the goals of Socratic seminars. Both foster deep habits of thought by challenging students to lead rather than follow. Both encourage students to take control of their own educations. Both are based on trust.

As educators, we constantly seek new ways to enhance our students' education. In particular, we seek classroom activities that foster students' inquiry and critical thinking skills. At Fremont High School, Socratic seminars have served as powerful and positive tools that have

Table 1

Class	Composition (Teacher-Graded)		Seminar (Self-Assessed)	
	Turn-In Percentage	Average Score	Turn-In Percentage	Average Score
Block I ENG 9	89	85	90	88
Block III ENG 9	92	88	92	89
Block IV ENG 9	83	86	84	83

encouraged the development of thoughtful and deeply inquisitive classrooms. Self-assessment has amplified this development and, thus far, our "leap of faith" into self-assessment has been successful.

Students also believe seminars are valuable. When approximately one hundred of our first-year English students were surveyed, seminars were selected as the most useful activity by nearly twice as many students as the second-place activity. In classroom discussion, they listed several reasons why this was so: Not only do seminars encourage close reading of a text, they also cause students to think deeply about challenging issues. Further, they create a safe, nonjudgmental environment in which students can speak and be heard. Seminars powerfully reinforce many positive behavioral messages that allow students to connect not just with a text or a teacher, but with each other. Finally, seminars target a wide range of the "essential skills" mandated by state departments of education.

In addition, students enjoy seminars. When first-year English students at Fremont were asked what class activity was their favorite, seminar was selected by more than a four-to-one margin over its nearest competitor. Students offered several reasons:

1. Seminars give them a chance to interact and to voice their opinions.

2. They also open students to a wide range of viewpoints, thus deepening their appreciation for a piece of literature.

3. The seminar and self-assessment process affords students a rare opportunity to self-direct their education and take responsibility for their own performance.

4. Finally, seminars are fun.

Works Cited

Bloom, Benjamin S. *Taxonomy of Educational Objectives: The Classification of Educational Goals. Handbook 1: Cognitive Domain.* New York: McKay, 1956.

Lambright, Lesley. "Dialogue and Discussion." *Socratic Seminars: Thought, Civility, Renewal, Connections.* Ed. Burt Plumb and John Ludy. Markle, IN: Region 8 Publications, 2000. 48.

Paul, Richard, and J. A. Binker. "Socratic Questioning." *Socratic Seminars: Thought, Civility, Renewal, Connections.* Ed. Burt Plumb and John Ludy. Markle, IN: Region 8 Publications, 2000. 50–58.

Appendix: Suggestions for Further Reading

1. *Critical Encounters in High School English: Teaching Literary Theory to Adolescents*, by Deborah Appleman. Urbana, IL: National Council of Teachers of English; and New York: Teachers College P, 2000.

   English teachers, buy this book right now, for it will give you the courage to try something you have perhaps always wanted to try—having students look through a particular literary theory lens as they read a text. Appleman (a former high school English teacher and now professor of educational studies and the liberal arts at Carleton College in Northfield, Minnesota), provides vignettes from actual classrooms to illustrate how teachers use particular lenses of critical theory to show students how a text can be read in a variety of ways. Arguing that "Critical lenses provide students with a way of reading their world . . . a way of 'seeing' differently and analytically" (3), Appleman advocates teaching students how to read literature with four different lenses: reader-response, Marxist, feminist, and deconstructionist. What's especially appealing about the book is that it includes suggested additional readings at the end of each chapter (all annotated), a list of selected literary texts one might use, and a wonderful appendix containing twenty-two activities for teachers to try.

2. *The Habit of Thought: From Socratic Seminars to Socratic Practice*, by Michael Strong. Chapel Hill, NC: New View, 1997.

   As Michael Strong notes in his introduction, Socratic practice "is more general than Junior Great Books or Touchstones, [which are] packaged curricula with specific rules for leading discussions" (1). Instead, it is an approach to classroom conversation directed toward the development of reading and thinking abilities in children in grades four and up, an approach in which the teacher/leader has no specific lesson plan or content in mind. The goal is a heightened understanding of the text as the community of learners "gives birth to their ideas by means of [the teacher's] questions" (61). Modeled in part on the discussion-leader-as-tutor-rather-than-professor tradition at St. John's College in Annapolis, Maryland, this is a program which employs ordinary conversation in helping students develop rigorous "habits of mind."

Strong's book includes chapters on intellectual integrity, on four models for integrating Socratic seminars into content-driven classrooms, and on how to use Socratic practice in organizing one's classroom. The appendixes provide a class participation assessment rubric, procedures for leading a Socratic seminar, and a list of excellent resources for implementation, such as the Touchstones Project, Junior Great Books, St. John's College, the National Paideia Center, and the Coalition for Essential Schools. Finally, the book advocates using "Socratic inquiry in the study of texts to develop the habit of thinking carefully" (4).

3. *Inquiry-Based English Instruction: Engaging Students in Life and Literature*, by Richard Beach and Jamie Myers. New York: Teachers College P, 2001.

Beach and Myers illustrate how social worlds are constructed, negotiated, maintained, and contested through literacy, language, media, and all forms of symbolic interaction. They maintain that how we speak, dress, gesture, listen to music, and use a variety of texts provide the symbolic tools through which we interact and interpret one another and the world.

The book gives a number of examples generated in a "social worlds" unit taught in a ninth-grade English class at State College High School in Pennsylvania. Students created print-based and media-based projects and products as they inquired into the nature of social worlds in their own lives and in the lives of characters from short stories in an anthology titled *Coming of Age: Short Stories about Youth and Adolescence,* edited by Bruce Emra. The students' work grew out of a focus on the following topics: "Families and Friends," "Falling in Love," "Out in the World," and "Do I Fit In?"

Perhaps most interesting to readers will be the emphasis on how new media (particularly hypertext and hypermedia) enlarge the possibilities for making meaning. Beach and Myers show how students linked photos, video, art, audio, and text to create interactive media experiences. They describe a curricular framework for English language arts classrooms, one that concentrates on six inquiry strategies which relate to the topic of social worlds: immersing, identifying, contextualizing, representing, critiquing, and transforming.

If you want to see how English teachers can use new media to foster inquiry, go to www.ed.psu.edu/k-12/socialworlds to view some of the movie projects students created.

4. *In Search of Understanding: The Case for Constructivist Classrooms*, by Jacqueline Grennon Brooks and Martin G. Brooks. Alexandria, VA: Association for Supervision and Curriculum Development, 1993.

If you have time to read only one book about constructivist theory and learning, this is the one to choose. The authors state the basic premise of constructivism in the opening chapter: "we construct our own understandings of the world in which we live" (4). In addition, they identify contrasts between traditional and constructivist classrooms, describe at length the guiding principles of constructivism, and conclude with a focus on how to become a constructivist teacher. For teachers who value inquiry learning, a constructivist classroom is right up their alley, for it emphasizes such notions as these: students pursuing their own questions, students viewed as thinkers with emerging theories about the world, teachers actively seeking students' points of view, and teachers adapting the curriculum to address students' suppositions (17).

5. *Literature as Exploration*, by Louise M. Rosenblatt. New York: Noble, 1968.

Louise Rosenblatt is the mother of reader-response theories of teaching literature, for it was she who argued that teachers should move literature teaching from a New Criticism focus to an understanding that readers bring highly divergent responses to their reading of a book. In the 1968 foreword to this seminal work, James R. Squire calls it Rosenblatt's "magnum opus," stating that it is "one of the very few books on the teaching of English that I believe all teachers should read" (vi). Without equivocating, Rosenblatt calls on readers to make a personal engagement with the text: "But all the student's knowledge about literary history, about authors and periods and literary types, will be so much useless baggage if he has not been led primarily to seek in literature a vital personal experience" (59).

It is no accident that a number of the writers in this book have referenced *Literature as Exploration*, for it has had enormous influence on the teaching of English and on practices such as Literature Circles and constructivism. For follow-up reading, try Rosenblatt's 1978 work, *The Reader, the Text, the Poem: The Transactional Theory of the Literary Work* (Carbondale, IL: Southern Illinois UP).

6. *Literature Circles: Voice and Choice in the Student-Centered Classroom*, by Harvey Daniels. York, ME: Stenhouse, 1994.

> Another idea that sprouted up from Louise Rosenblatt's reader-response notion that "a text is just ink on a page until a reader comes along and gives it life" (qtd. in Daniels 34), Literature Circles give students opportunities to be more responsible for their own education, to become lifelong readers, and, in Daniels's words, to "nurture a critical, personal stance toward ideas" (31). Daniels describes Literature Circles as a new-old idea that employs features of cooperative learning and student-centeredness. Key aspects typically include most or all of the following, among others: students choosing their own reading materials, small groups forming based on book choice, groups meeting on a regular schedule to discuss their reading, students using written notes to guide their reading and discussion, discussion topics coming from the students, group meetings aiming for an open conversation about the books, students playing a rotating assortment of roles, the teacher serving as a facilitator and not a group member, assessment including evaluation by teacher observation and student self-evaluation (18).
>
> The spirit of inquiry is alive and well in the Literature Circles approach when it is successful, and this book can teach you how to use this method. Chapters address getting started, scheduling and managing groups, developing materials and role sheets to use (some even in Spanish), record keeping/evaluation/grading, and problems and questions. Two chapters on teachers' applications (for primary/intermediate grades *and* middle school through college) are particularly helpful, and there is an excellent references section.

7. *On the Brink: Negotiating Literature and Life with Adolescents*, by Susan Hynds. New York: Teachers College P, 1997.

> This is a worthy account of how English teachers wrestle with the "knowledge or growth" tension in teaching. Hynds, a former secondary English teacher and now professor of English education, talks about the schizophrenic behavior that often plagues English teachers who "adopt holistic, learner-centered approaches to writing, for example, but still cling to transmissionist approaches to literature teaching such as basal readers at the elementary level and worksheets or study questions at the secondary level" (7). Acknowledging the social nature of language learning, Hynds began studying adolescent readers with a particular interest in the social construing abilities of readers. Aided by a grant from the NCTE Research Foundation, she embarked on a two-year

study with a seventh-grade teacher in a Northeastern city. This study, focusing particularly on eight students, revealed the teacher's frustrations in trying to implement a learner-centered approach (trying to do "too much, too soon"). But the teacher persevered, gradually incorporating techniques such as Literature Circles and a choice-centered/individualized curriculum into her classroom with success.

This is a useful book for those who seek to move from a teacher-centered instructional model to a performance-centered, learner-centered constructivist classroom.

8. *The Paideia Program: An Educational Syllabus: Essays by the Paideia Group,* edited and with a preface and introduction by Mortimer J. Adler. New York: Macmillan, 1984.

This last book of the trilogy written by members of the Paideia group—the other two being *The Paideia Proposal: An Educational Manifesto* (Macmillan, 1982) and *Paideia Problems and Possibilities* (Macmillan, 1983)—is intended for teachers who want to try Paideia teaching in their schools and classrooms. Adler, noted philosopher, educator, and Great Books founder, sets forth a review of the distinctive features of the Paideia program in his introduction. Paideia is a general course of study for all students in grades K–12, one in which the three modes of teaching are didactic instruction, coaching, and Socratic questioning (described in the opening chapter by Adler, Charles Van Doren, and Theodore Sizer). The following ten chapters illustrate how one might teach the various subject matters in a curriculum. Of particular interest will be the chapter written by Geraldine Van Doren on English language and literature. There is also a final section on how a Paideia school should be structured, a chapter on grading, and an appendix containing recommended readings for seminars and other discussions for students in grades K–12.

9. *"You Gotta BE the Book": Teaching Engaged and Reflective Reading with Adolescents,* by Jeffrey D. Wilhelm. Urbana, IL: National Council of Teachers of English; and New York: Teachers College P, 1997.

It's not surprising that this is one of the most popular titles listed in the NCTE catalog, as it provides both a theoretical background and practical tips for those who soon will or already do teach adolescent readers. Michael W. Smith, in his foreword, says this about the book: "Jeff Wilhelm does something that no other teacher or theorist or researcher of whom I am aware does: he articulates a powerful theory of literary reading grounded on the reading of students and he uses that theory to build a powerful theory of the teaching of literature" (xi). Studying nine students for a full year, Wilhelm tells us that success in reading depends on the reader's ability to enter into and become involved in a story world. Thus engaged, students need to find ways to articulate what they feel and understand about the books they read.

Wilhelm found that using drama and drawing often freed up even the most reluctant readers to talk about books. Ultimately, his goal was to create a reader-centered classroom, one using a "bottom-up" rather than a "top-down" approach. For thirteen years as a secondary teacher, Wilhelm kept a journal about his teaching experiences, recording observations about particular students, assessing what worked or didn't work, noting his theories, and revising his lessons. During the year in which he conducted his research, the author employed techniques such as the following: literary letters which students exchanged with other students and with Wilhelm, symbolic story representations (students created cutouts or found objects to dramatize what they read), and think-aloud protocols (some spoken into a tape recorder, some written, and some drawn as pictures).

All of these tactics were designed to help students take ownership of their reading, get away from the teacher-knows-best model we know so well, and become more engaged with the text. Appendixes include questions and activities for what Wilhelm calls the "dimensions of reader response" as well as revolving role drama lessons for Sheila Every Burnford's *The Incredible Journey*. You gotta be the book, and you gotta read the book, particularly if you believe students have the ability to be reading experts themselves.

Index

Editors

Harmon's Photography, Northfield, MN

James Holden retired in 2001 after seven and one-half years as assistant professor of education at St. Olaf College in Northfield, Minnesota. During his years at St. Olaf, he taught, among other courses, English methods and first-year writing classes. In addition, he supervised many preservice English teachers during their twelve weeks of student teaching. He also taught four years in the education department at Gustavus Adolphus College in St. Peter, Minnesota, and taught high school and junior high school English for twenty-nine years—for twenty of those years at Northfield High School in Northfield, Minnesota. He has written or co-authored three articles on the topic of Socratic seminars, particularly with a focus on having students prepare questions to lead their own discussions. Married for forty years to Caroline, Holden has two grown children (both also teachers) and three grandchildren. He loves to fly-fish for trout and play tennis. In fact, he is writing a book about coaching tennis in cold weather climates called *Tennis on the Tundra: A Short Season.*

John S. Schmit is associate professor of English at Augsburg College in Minneapolis, where he has taught linguistics, writing, American literature, and cognitive science since 1990. A former director of Augsburg's Paideia Program, he also serves as a faculty member in the Carleton College Summer Writing Program—a three-week program for high school writers—and conducts workshops for AP language and composition teachers. His research interests include assessment of writing and applications of linguistics in the analysis of literature. He is also associate dean for adult programs, overseeing a range of educational opportunities for working adults.

Contributors

Richard Beach is Wallace Professor of English Education at the University of Minnesota. He is author of *A Teacher's Introduction to Reader-Response Theories* and coauthor of *Teaching Literature in the Secondary School*. He conducts research on response to literature, composition, and inquiry instruction, and is a member of the board of directors of the National Reading Conference.

Elizabeth A. City is a doctoral student in administration, planning, and social policy at the Harvard Graduate School of Education. A member of the National Paideia Faculty, she has also been the co-director of a Paideia school and has taught secondary humanities, English, and Spanish. Her research interests include classroom discourse, leadership, and school transformation.

Martha Strom Cosgrove has been a teacher of English language arts since 1973, working with a variety of student populations including adult learners. She currently teaches American literature and advanced placement courses at Edina High School in Edina, Minnesota. As English department chair, Cosgrove has spearheaded curricular changes in language arts, including the incorporation of literary theory into high school course work. Having recently completed work for National Board Certification, she is presently focusing on an innovative breakfast reading club to help students share her lifelong passion for recreational reading.

Sharon Eddleston has been a secondary English teacher for more than thirty years. She received her Ph.D. from the University of Minnesota in 1998. Her dissertation focused on whole-class discussions of literature.

Mark Ensrud is an English teacher at Northfield High School in Northfield, Minnesota, where he teaches English 9 and college prep writing classes. He also works part of the day as a media specialist at the high school and is currently working on his master's in guidance counseling. He graduated from Gustavus Adolphus College in St. Peter, Minnesota, in 1994 and is a member of NCTE, the Minnesota Council of Teachers of English (MCTE), and Phi Beta Kappa.

Mark Gellis is a 1993 graduate of Purdue University in Indiana (Ph.D. in English/rhetoric and composition). He is presently associate professor of communication in the Department of Liberal Studies at Kettering University in Flint, Michigan, where he teaches technical and professional writing, speech, and literature. His recent publications include "Teaching Research Skills Using the Internet" in *Issues in Web-Based Pedagogy: A Critical Primer* (edited by Robert A. Cole) and "The

Rhetoric of George Campbell's Sermons" in *Scottish Rhetoric and Its Influences* (edited by Lynee Lewis Gaillet). His research interests include pedagogy, rhetorical criticism, and Internet-based communication.

Michael S. Hale is assistant professor in the College of Education at Appalachian State University in Boone, North Carolina. A member of the National Paideia Faculty, he has also been co-director of a Paideia charter school and taught social studies and humanities in grades 6–12. His research interests include classroom discourse, dialogic instruction, teacher development, and school change.

Elfie Israel, a graduate of Barnard College, earned an M.A. from New York University and an Ed.D. from Nova Southeastern University. She is currently in charge of professional development at Pembroke Pines Charter High School in Pembroke Pines, Florida, where she also chairs the English department and teaches one class of AP English. In addition, she is adjunct professor at St. Leo University in St. Leo, Florida, where she trains teachers of the gifted. She is also a College Board trainer of AP English and vertical teams, and, as a member of the Florida League of Teachers, she is actively involved in mentoring teachers in the state. She has taught in public and private schools in New York, the Bahamas, and Florida. For three years, she was coeditor of *Florida English Journal*. Her articles on teaching have been published in *English Journal, Florida English Journal*, and the *Eric Digest*. She has just completed writing a book on Advanced Placement English literature for students.

John N. Ludy teaches English at Fremont High School in Fremont, Indiana. He is a nationally recognized Socratic seminar facilitator-trainer and adjunct professor of education at Indiana University South Bend.

G. Douglas Meyers is professor of English at the University of Texas at El Paso, where he recently helped to create a new Master of Arts in the Teaching of English degree. In 2000 Meyers received the university's highest honor bestowed upon faculty, the Distinguished Achievement Award for Teaching Excellence. Meyers has also taught at the University of Maryland (where he earned his doctorate) and Florida International University, and he has published extensively in the areas of composition/rhetoric and English education, which continue to be his primary research interests.

Barbara G. Pace is assistant professor of English education at the University of Florida. Before joining the faculty at UF, she taught English in the Florida public schools and in college. Her research interests are focused on the role of discursive processes in classrooms and online communities. She is interested in how social roles are maintained and challenged and how classroom talk supports learning. She has published on these issues in *English Journal*, the *New Advocate*, and the *International Journal of Qualitative Studies in Education*, among others.

Raymond A. Philippot is assistant professor of English education at St. Cloud State University in St. Cloud, Minnesota. He taught secondary English in Wichita, Kansas, and Fergus Falls, Minnesota. His research interests include teacher development, classroom discussion, and response to literature.

Burt Plumb is a consultant on Socratic seminars with the Indiana Department of Education. He is also adjunct professor of education for Indiana University South Bend.

Jacqueline S. Thursby is assistant professor in the English department at Brigham Young University in Provo, Utah. She teaches upper division classes in secondary English methods, folklore, and literature/myth/folkloristics. She has published one book, *Mother's Table, Father's Chair: Cultural Narratives of Basque American Women*, and several articles on secondary English and language arts, folklore, ethnography, and cemetery studies. Her research interests are varied, ranging from continued ethnographic research among the Basque American people and ongoing studies in American cemetery and funerary lore, to research in secondary classroom methodologies using folklore and literature in combination for classroom discussion.

Jane S. Townsend is associate professor in the area of language and literacy at the University of Florida in Gainesville. Her teaching interests center on language use in the classroom, and her research includes work on classroom discourse and students' and teachers' understanding of linguistic diversity. She has published articles on these topics in *English Education, English Journal*, and *Language Arts*, among others. She is coeditor of *Teaching Language Arts: Learning Through Dialogue* (1999).

This book was typeset in Palatino and Helvetica by Electronic Imaging.
The typefaces used on the cover were Book Antigua, Palatino, and Univers Condensed.
The book was printed on 50-lb. Husky Offset by IPC Communication Services.